PAIN UNSEEN

PAIN
UNSEEN

The Truths That Lie Beneath My Strength

CASEY
RICHARDSON

Foreword by Rosalind Hudnell

To Corey – the greatest constant in my life.

Freeing yourself was one thing;

claiming ownership of that freed self was another.

- *Toni Morrison,* Beloved, *1987*

FOREWORD

Rosalind Hudnell

"You are my role model. You inspire me." As I sat down with Casey for the first time, I was struck with how deeply she made eye contact, saying words that I have been honored to hear from many before. It was something about the way she said them that seemed to touch me differently. Her smile and the way she embraced me felt genuine, without any pretense or camouflage. She conveyed her soul in a way that I could feel. Her willingness to be vulnerable in such an intimate way made me realize that some of my own walls seemed to evaporate in that moment. There was no reason for maintaining boundaries; it felt as if we had known each other forever. As she began to talk about how she had followed my journey, I couldn't help but stare into what appeared to be the soul of my younger self. I knew in that moment that she had to tell her story. She had discovered her own secret of joy far younger than I did, and I knew that her ability to thrive would take her even further. I also knew that by finding her voice, she would help others do the same.

Pain Unseen chronicles one woman's journey of life through pain, a journey which far too many of us have traveled. Deeply personal and raw, it examines how navigating and responding to life experiences can shape the paths we are destined to follow. Not necessarily a how-to book, but one that does teach, Casey has done a remarkable job of exemplifying how fragility can give way to strength, courage, and success. From beginning to end, readers will come to see how examining critical decisions made by the adults who raised us, the people who chose to love us, and our own, can lead to the truth of our existence.

This book will shatter a principle that many of us were taught, to just "grin and bear it." The belief that our legacy of pain is something to hide, to be used as a shield of armor. As Casey states, "I learned to step over pain early in my life." Her writing will pierce your soul in ways that are likely to help shed false perceptions and narratives of what strength looks like. As she conveys her emotional breakdown, you will find yourself fighting for her triumph as she relinquishes herself to the pain and recognizes the importance of seeking and accepting help. As a result, we are taken on a journey through the unimaginable, witnessing the triumph of what happens when our fear turns into the fuel for our courage.

Every day, millions of people start their day hiding so much pain beneath the surface and, like an iceberg, only a portion of who they are is visible. We judge each other by labels enforced by our job titles, education, and social status, and yet beneath the surface is where our greatest commonality as human beings is found. True depictions of people are complex, imperfect, and filled with disappointments, which in a more inclusive and empathetic world we would be more comfortable sharing. There is far too much faking going on, contributing to increased stress, illness and overall dissatisfaction. We are often encouraged by our workplaces to bring our full selves to work, but most remain too afraid to test whether it is truly acceptable to do so. Becoming real is a heroic, yet terrifying act.

Pain Unseen is one writer's attempt to shed light on the reality that what you see is often not what is real. We all have times where our smile is hiding the fear, fatigue, and pain struggling to surface, yet all the while creating danger for those who get the closest, especially ourselves. After reading this book you will forever be reminded that when we encounter women, particularly black women who are achieving success with confidence, strength, and capability, it didn't come easily. Women are born with an inherent sense of survival and strength, but for many that instinct is destroyed as a result of physical and mental abuse. From that point forward, no matter what we become and what we do, the ultimate challenge and daily internal struggle is to reclaim our power. Many are in fact still walking into the workplace, the classroom, and on stages trying their best to cover their insecurities, struggles, and pain.

This book will take you on the journey of how one woman worked her way through her own illusions to doing the work necessary to reclaim her strength and making that her newfound reality. It may sound like a cliché, but it's real. Until we really are free, we cannot soar. I am honored to be this author's mentor and role model, and through her story I have found my own renewed inspiration. My hope is that her journey will inspire others to chart their own and help others do the same. *Pain Unseen* is a wonderful place to start.

CONTENTS

PROLOGUE

June 28, 2016
2:40 p.m.

I've just taken a walk along the pier in San Francisco and am now seated on a wooden bench facing the Bay. Across the water I can see Alcatraz. Wow. Perched in front of me, resting without a hint of fear, are two white birds standing on the wooden rail of the pier. In front of me lies such a beautiful scene of serenity. I can hear the waves in the water… swishing as the wind blows. I close my eyes and dare to take a moment to relax for a quick second. I dare to just "be" for a moment, enjoying the present.

This inhalation and slow exhalation… this peace… this acknowledgement of the present moment lasts all of three seconds and then I am fully awake. I hear the zooming of cars to my left. Steps ahead, the loud chatter of people as they flood the streets heading to and from Fisherman's Wharf. The beckoning of tour salesmen enticing people to take a boat ride to visit the infamous Alcatraz. I see couples holding hands. I see young teens walking with earphones, bopping their heads. I smell aromas of food nearby… fresh baked bread, Vietnamese cuisine, and fried seafood served from booths along the street. I am awake. Life is still moving. I, too, must continue to move.

I am a twenty-six-year-old, successful finance professional. An assertive, inquisitive, and passionate individual. A mentor to women and young, underrepresented minorities. A singer and lover of neo-soul, hiphop, and jazz. I have been a rock to so many people in my life. I'm an empath with a deep interest in helping others see the very best of themselves. I love pulling out people's strengths. That has always been my leadership style – leading and healing through empowering. I've always been on a mission to help those often marginalized. To help them rise in a world not necessarily structured to aid in their success. To liberate minds and help people see beyond what even their closest surroundings assert as being possible. I have always been drawn to that calling.

I have always been drawn to this because, while others wouldn't naturally assume this, I was the perfect case study. I've always known that if I could navigate the terrains of loss, instability, and abandonment while conquering the adversity of rigor and competition – others could do the same. I believed that if I could study the formula for what made a person successful... if I could exhibit the characteristics of those who occupied the spaces that I desired, I could be just as successful. And others could do the same.

But, at twenty-six years old, I'm starting my life over in a new city that I've never set foot in. I've traveled 2,700 miles on a one-way flight to escape what was once home. I've abandoned everything – my family, my friends, my teammates, my house, my mentors, my church, and my routines. I've done all of this because sixteen days ago, my husband of four years abused me.

I'm standing on the pier, trying to steady myself and find a place to pack the pain. I have to move on. My success and my dreams depend on it. In only a week's time, I need to somehow arrive to my new San Francisco office building, unscathed and wearing a smile.

1

THE SHATTERING

"Pieces of me were scattered, blowing in the cold. In different directions… truth be told." – Jill Scott, "Back Together"

I left the room completely untouched for nine days. For nine days, I left it as it was so that I could remember. So that I would not forget what actually happened. So that the actions that took place that night would not be altered. So that my love for my husband would not compel me to downplay the horror that played out that night. So that I did not allow his messages and pleading to suffocate the resolve that I had built up.

There are distinctions of that room that remain vivid in my mind today.

The loft. Immediately to the left of a winding wooden staircase, the loft was a mess. A tall oscillating fan was knocked over, its broken pieces scattered across the carpet. So many little pieces.

The curtains. Thrown to the side of the windowsills, they were no longer neatly draped to the floor. Instead, they were haphazardly cast aside.

The blanket. Twisted around the floor and stretched in a random sort of way… it likely tussled around as feet struggled on top of it. A result of stumbling from one end of the room to the other.

I wanted to remember that night. I wanted to see the room exactly as it was after I was attacked by my husband. I still don't understand what caused him to become so enraged, violent even. To approach me with such a vicious intensity. I still can't understand it.

"Hit me so I can beat your motherfucking ass," he kept shouting in my face – his face so close to mine that our noses collided.

He wasn't satisfied with the choking, pressing his thumb directly onto my throat, restricting the air from my lungs. He wasn't satisfied with thrusting my body into the walls and the windows. So much so that my arms, back, and legs were visibly bruised from his tight grip. He wasn't satisfied with slamming me against the windowsill and various objects in the room. I knew that he would not be satisfied until he was able to truly hurt me. To strike me with his fists.

"Hit me so I can beat your motherfucking ass," he must have yelled over ten times.

He wanted to feel justified. There was a rage inside him that he so desperately wanted to relieve. He was almost pleading for me to hit him back, though the urgency in his voice did not quite reflect the cold fury in his eyes.

It had been such a long year. He had somehow

lost three jobs, contributing to his downward spiral into substance abuse. What's more, I had agreed to counseling a few months prior in attempt at reconciliation after discovering his infidelity.

I had just let Aaron know that our marriage was over. I wasn't shouting or enraged; instead, I was numb. And tired. I was so tired and over it. I told him that I knew that he was still communicating with the other woman. He initially denied it and then stated that he had only been checking on her because he felt guilty about abruptly ending their relationship.

I picked up his cell phone from the middle armrest of the couch when he suddenly lunged on top of me, choking me with both his hands.

Like so many other unrecognizable characteristics I had witnessed in Aaron over the past year – I had never experienced violence from him. I could barely recognize the man that I fell in love with. No matter what he did, I would not strike him back. Judging from the look in his eyes, I knew if I did, he would hurt me even worse than he already had.

His fury continued, and after a while he threw me

into the corner of the loft, right at the top of the wooden staircase. My back crashed into a corner of the windowsill, and I moaned from the pain.

"Yeah, yeah," he said with an angry smirk. "You can't beat me! Try me! You can't beat me!"

Aaron wanted to feel dominant. To forcibly reclaim something that he felt was slipping through his fingers. Beneath those eyes that I could barely recognize, I knew that there was also brokenness and pain.

He grabbed my arms and yelled, "I am going to throw you down the fucking stairs." Horrified, I quickly grabbed the curtains and held on for dear life.

Flashes of what my mother must have felt on the day of her murder flooded through my head. My mother, at twenty-one years old, was murdered. While in her own apartment complex selling Avon products. In a place that I'm sure she felt some sense of safety and security. Since she lived there.

I lived here.

I couldn't believe this was happening to me. I

couldn't believe that he and I were in this moment. Enacting this form of horror. It was surreal. To think of all the things he hated from his childhood... to think of the very people he resented because of the same acts, I couldn't believe he would resort himself to the same behavior.

My hands gripped the curtains tightly as Aaron continued to grab my body from different angles to attempt to throw me down the staircase. Arms. Then torso. Then legs. Pulling me as I pulled the curtains.

As we tussled, I managed to throw him back. I attempted to run away from the corner to make it to the full floor of the loft. I made it a few steps before he yanked me and began to thrust my body over the banister overlooking the drop of the stairs. The banister with iron rods. Those iron rods bent as the weight of my body pressed against them. I tried to push away as my husband continued to press me forward.

In my mind, I just knew the banister would snap and I would tumble down headfirst, breaking my neck and an arm at the very least. He pressed, and I pushed away until I finally wriggled out of his hold.

Overwhelmed with gratitude, I thanked God that the banister did not snap from the wooded base, as it surely could have. Only God could have prevented it, because in my husband's rage, he was stronger than I'd ever seen. His force was so strong... and equally as hateful.

Eventually, I was able to text an acquaintance from the adjacent neighborhood, asking her to quickly pick me up. She did, and while at her house, I called the police. They arrived, and I recounted the events. Though I was visibly battered and crying, I asked the police to remove my husband from our home but not to arrest him.

"I don't want him to have a record," I said. "He's in a dark place right now after losing a few jobs. But I want him to have a chance to get his life back on track, and it's going to be hard for him to do so with a record. Please... get him out of the house, but do not arrest him."

There are people who cringe at my decision to ask the policemen to refrain from arresting my husband, but it was the choice I made out of love. Though I knew I was done with the marriage and resolute in my stance, I wanted my husband to have a chance to find himself. I understood that he would need the chance to push through the pain and trauma in his life. My thought – even in that moment – was to show grace and allow him space to get back on the right track one day, though it would have to be without me.

After returning home, the police let me know that when they showed up to the house, Aaron had his arms extended, admitting, "I deserve to go to jail for what I just did."

They told him he was lucky to have a wife who was looking out for him and that she had declined pressing charges so that he could get a decent job in the future. The police shook their heads, telling me they had walked up to where the incident took place and, from the looks of that room, they thought he absolutely should have been in jail that night. I stood by my decision and thanked them for honoring it.

That night, and every night for the next nine days, I slept safely in the homes of friends. I would go back to the house to gather the things I needed, each time leaving the loft area exactly as it was from the night of the incident. I refused to repaint the picture of how the room looked. I did not want to downplay the events of that night. For a full nine days following the incident, I left that area of the house untouched, exactly as it was.

As I usually do in the face of negative circumstance, I busied myself. I changed the locks on the doors, replaced the garage door openers, and purchased and installed blinds to cover the bare glass windows and door. That was the first twenty-four hours. I returned to work after one day off... attempting to get back to normalcy. That was my plan. To sit in positions throughout the workday where I couldn't feel the soreness in my back and arms. To not let pain show on my face when I would move in ways that strained me.

I remember the team meeting I sat in the morning that I returned to work. Every second that went by felt like hours. Throughout the meeting, all I could concentrate on was holding back tears as I struggled to ignore flashes of the abuse replaying in my head and to endure the tenderness I felt all over my body. I tried to make it through that day, but it was impossible to maintain focus.

My husband was emailing my work mailbox nonstop. He called my office phone over and over again. I received so many text messages, one ominously stating, "I am not living without you." In that moment, I could no longer disguise my fear.

I jumped up, in a panic, and went to my team's admin. I told her that I needed to step out to find a lawyer immediately. That I needed to get a restraining order, and I needed to leave right then. She was flustered, but told me to take care of what I needed and that she'd be waiting by her phone on standby if I required anything.

I left immediately and found a lawyer who could see me that day. Once I arrived at the lawyer's office, I told him everything that had happened and that I needed to get a restraining order as quickly as possible. The lawyer gave me very clear instructions on where to go – directing me to the courthouse just a few blocks away. He told me what floor to go to, what paperwork to request, and what to say when I submitted my paperwork to the representative at the acceptance window.

He advised that I would receive a temporary restraining order protection the same day, which would last through the date of my scheduled court hearing. He explained that the court hearing date would be set while I stood at that same window and that on the day of my hearing, after explaining my case, the judge would grant a one-year restraining order.

He further explained that the state of North Carolina required legal separation for a full year in order for divorce to be granted. This requirement was true whether abuse had occurred in the marriage or not. He highlighted that the yearlong restraining order would coincide with the one-year separation requirement, given that the day that the police removed my husband from our home was the day that my separation began.

The lawyer laid out all these details in a very

matter-of-fact manner, which was startling as well as sobering. We were speaking rather directly about the crumbling of a decade-long relationship. The shattering of two lives that had been meticulously threaded together.

Yet I needed to execute my decision efficiently and effectively, so as to cause as little disruption to my life and job as possible. As I'd asked, the lawyer had presented everything I needed to attain a restraining order... in a few short sentences. He made it clear how things needed to flow if I was ready to act on leaving.

I did exactly as the lawyer instructed and received the temporary restraining order that same day. The court case was scheduled to occur eight days later. My phone, however, did not stop buzzing. Aaron's messages had become more and more desperate. The messages included threats of suicide if I did not talk to him.

I felt dizzy from all that was happening in my life at that time. I gave my best friend, Monnie, a call. I'll never forget the words from her that stopped me in my tracks.

"Casey, you can't possibly be planning to stay in that house. You can't think you'll be safe there."

She was right. It hit me – he knew where I lived, we built that house together from the ground up. He knew where I worked, he knew where I parked my car. He knew who my family members were – their phone numbers and where they lived. We had been together for close to ten years, I could never be safe from him.

I realized that I would be looking over my shoulder for the foreseeable future. Even with a piece of paper saying that I was protected, I was not safe. It wasn't just the house that we shared, it was my life. My entire life.

As I considered these things, I decided that I owed it to myself to feel safe. To not have to look over my shoulder. To not be cornered. To not live in fear. I quickly pondered the places that I could go and still have a vibrant career while also being far out of reach. New York and San Francisco both came to mind. New York was fast-paced and gritty. From accounts that I had been told, San Francisco was likely a happy-medium between Charlotte (where I lived) and New York.

It dawned on me that I had a family friend who lived in the Bay Area. Someone who my husband didn't know well at all. He would never guess that I would move to the Bay Area with her.

After what may have been mere seconds, but felt like an hour, I responded to Monnie.

"You're right. I'm going to have to move. I'm going to have to leave for my safety. I am moving to California. Right after my restraining order is granted next week, I'm moving to California."

When I walked back into my office building, I pulled aside a newly promoted vice president on my team by the name of Phillip. I had grown to trust his opinion, and I needed a quick sounding board from a person I respected in my office. I told him what had happened to me in the days prior. I shared the unsettling dynamics that I was dealing with at that moment and my plan to move to San Francisco so as to not lose steam in my career but still be safely out of reach. While confiding in him, I remember watching his expression turn from rage to sadness, then eventually to reassurance.

He looked me intently in my eyes and said, "Casey, I have no doubts that you can pull this off."

Phillip repeatedly apologized for what I had experienced, expressing his sincere disappointment and sadness around the circumstance. He told me that I undoubtedly had a bright future ahead of me and that I was doing right by myself to seek safety and to secure a good future.

I let out a huge sigh. His words were a symbolic hug that felt vitally important at that moment. All of this was so much – forty-eight hours had changed the entire course of my life. Yet as drastic as my decision was, I had received reassurance that my quickly derived "plan of pivot" sounded solid.

I asked Phillip his thoughts on what our managing director would say when I went in to reveal all this. I told him that I understood how our industry had a, "What can you do for me today?" climate and that I didn't expect there to be much leniency offered around my plans to depart. Regardless, I told him, I was walking away from Charlotte to secure my future and my safety.

Phillip looked at me and said, "Casey, don't assume that you can't ask for what you need. I believe that you can work remotely. You're valued. You need to be safe. Ask for what you need."

After our chat, I walked into my managing director's office and asked him if he had a few minutes to talk with me about something very urgent. He looked at me with much concern and replied yes. I opened my mouth to speak and tears came flooding down my face. Up until this point in the day, I had managed to remain poised. So calculated. But in this moment, the weight of what had happened to me and the change I was making in my life was extremely heavy, too heavy to ignore.

I let my managing director know that my husband had abused me; that his behavior had become so unrecognizable and irrational that I was fearful for my safety. I told him that I had decided to move to San Francisco with a family friend immediately following my court hearing – which had been scheduled for the following Wednesday.

I admitted that my actions were not ideal for the team and that I did not expect him to hold my job for me long-term, but I mentioned that if he would be willing to allow me to work remotely up until September, I would figure things out and find a permanent job for myself elsewhere.

I told him that I needed to leave in order to be safe. I wasn't going to be looking over my shoulder every time I left the office to go to my car. I planned to move with my family friend in San Francisco, away from all of the obvious places that my husband would expect to find me. I told him that I needed the rest of that week and the week following to prepare for the move so that I could leave immediately after the court case. I explained that I would not be able to come into the office while I did so and that this was nonnegotiable for me. My life was more important to me at that moment than anything else.

I had done it. In a flurry of dropping so many heavy details, I had told my group head exactly what I needed. I was fully prepared for something adverse to happen. The variations of that possibility were so plentiful, I had no desire to play out what they could be. But to be honest, I didn't care in that moment. I believed enough in myself to leave and start over and be just fine – even if I was to start with no job. I knew this was what I had to do.

My managing director gave me his fullest support and deepest sympathy. He told me to leave, take care of everything that I needed, and that we would worry about the details of that later – but to go and do what I needed to do to be safe. He asked me to have someone to walk me to my car, and I did. That would be the last time I would see my managing director's face before my move.

In that moment, I learned so much about what it meant to be a leader. I learned that at the most important level – being human and standing in solidarity with a person is the most transformative power a person can lend. I am forever grateful to that managing director. I am forever grateful to Phillip, the vice president on my team.

Over the course of the next eight days, I secured the lawyer I had spoken to previously so that he could represent me in whatever way I might need over the next year. My lawyer confirmed that a move to San Francisco was absolutely allowed and that after a year of legal separation, I would be able to file for divorce.

I asked my lawyer what my options were for selling the house, and he told me that Aaron would have to sign the deed solely over to me in order for me to sell it. He drew up paperwork to have on hand at the court hearing in case Aaron would agree to sign such documents.

Phillip gave me a referral for a real estate agent, whom I called, explaining my circumstance. The agent agreed to be on standby up until after the court hearing – at which time I would know whether I had the legal right to put my house up for sale on my own.

I purchased a one-way plane ticket to fly to California the Friday after my court case. I gave myself a day's cushion between the hearing and my departure date to handle anything that I might need to, whether my husband signed the deed papers or not.

The days leading up to the hearing were scary. Calls and texts from Aaron were constant. After refusing to speak with him, he reached out to my family members, threatening to harm himself if I did not stay with him. One night, Aaron texted that he had loaded one bullet in the chamber of a gun and pulled the trigger against his temple a few times. He wrote that because the gun didn't fire, it was a sign that we were supposed to be together.

Whether or not Aaron was being honest about this attempt, it scared the shit out of me. What if he really did try to kill himself? What if he forced his way into my friend's home to find me and hurt someone in his desperation? How much uglier could this situation get, even if I did make it to Friday and board my flight?

One thing was for sure – none of these gestures made me second-guess my decision to leave. This was a nightmare and not to be underestimated. I needed to get out. To be safe. To protect myself.

The night before my hearing, my older brother, Corey, drove up from Florida to join me at the courthouse. He wanted to support me through the impending difficulty I was facing. Corey didn't doubt a single ounce of my "plan of pivot" – except for the fact that he believed my husband should have been in jail. Aside from that, he believed that I was making all the right decisions, and he was there to stand with me.

I returned to my house with Corey that night and went upstairs to finally reassemble the loft area. I wanted to prepare the house and set up things perfectly just in case I was able to call the realtor after the hearing. I picked up all the broken fragments from the carpet and removed the items that had been scattered across the floor. I straightened the curtains and blinds, then cleaned the entire room to make the space feel warm and inviting, as it was intended to be.

Seeing the room was painful. I stood near the staircase and sobbed as I thought back on what happened, as well as what was to happen over next few days. My "forever plan" had turned on its head so drastically. My entire life was about to change in the matter of a week's time.

On the morning of the court hearing, there were so many knots in my stomach. The pain in my chest was almost unbearable. And underneath it all there was undoubtedly a deep sadness in my heart. But I had to take care of Casey. I had to swallow that sadness and keep on moving.

As I approached the doors of the courtroom, I saw the silhouette of my husband, and everything inside me fell to my feet. Suddenly, my legs felt like lead. Aaron sat on a bench outside the courtroom beside his mother. He looked like he hadn't slept in days. There was so much sorrow in his eyes.

There was so much sorrow in my heart for us.

My brother must have felt the rhythm of my stride hesitate and said, "Come on, Casey, let's do this." My big brother had me. I let more of my weight rest on him. I let him help pull me forward. Arms locked together, Corey and I walked past my husband and mother-in-law, and we entered the courtroom.

Women were required to sit on the left side of the courtroom, and men were required to sit on the right. My brother protectively watched me until I sat down, and then he went over to take a seat on his respective side. As I sat listening to the cases called before mine, I felt so much for the victims as they recounted their tragedies. There was one woman who made a motion to retract her previous request for a restraining order and return to the arms of her abuser. I felt even more sorrow for her.

As I sat listening, my lawyer came up to me and said, "Casey, I'm sorry – but Aaron doesn't want to sign the paperwork for the deed."

Anger instantly rushed through my body. I couldn't believe that he would push back on signing the paperwork, knowing he was laid off at the time, which left me to continue to absorb the mortgage payment. The woman who he had abused and would no longer be with!

My lawyer walked away while I sat, furious. I pulled out my phone to vent to my dad and stepmom.

I told my parents how livid I was and how I wanted to march over to my husband and give him a piece of my mind!

As I was putting my phone back into my purse, my lawyer walked up to me again and said, "Casey, he came to me and said that he would sign the paperwork after all."

It turned out that Aaron was initially stunned that I had gone as far as securing a lawyer. He had a bit of a fit outside the courtroom – repeating how he knew it must really be over if I had gotten a lawyer. Though Aaron initially said that he didn't want to sign anything, he reapproached my lawyer, saying that he would sign the deed of the house over.

As my lawyer recounted everything, my rage subsided, and I knew that in as much pain as both of us were in – we loved one another. We both wanted what was best for the other person. Though I had decided that we would no longer be a unit, that our marriage was unhealthy for both of us, there was still a level of love that we genuinely shared. We would each have to follow through on our own, separate paths to get to a better state. The separation was absolutely necessary.

Our case was called. The judge read through the events as they were outlined in the police statements. My husband did not contest. The judge granted a one-year restraining order.

I turned to walk down the aisle towards the exit door of the courtroom and saw my mother- and sister-in-law's faces. They, too, looked as if they were in so much pain. I gave them both individual hugs and let them know that I loved them very much. I knew that these would be my last hugs with them. This would be my last time seeing them for the foreseeable future. They were my family. They had been part of my life for a decade. I loved them… very much. This, I knew, was goodbye.

I rejoined my lawyer and Corey, who were waiting on the right side of the courtroom. The three of us walked out of the courthouse together.

My lawyer gave me the paperwork that I needed to be able to put my house on the market, and I let him know that I was meeting with the realtor that evening, then catching a plane to the Bay Area that Friday.

He raised his eyebrow and said, "Well then. Best wishes in California. We will talk in a year if nothing else goes awry."

I had the realtor come over late that evening. We signed paperwork and rearranged furniture to stage the home for potential homebuyers. We talked through how we would handle the listing process virtually. The realtor wished me luck, and we shook hands before he departed.

I had done it. I had stuck to my resolve and would be saying goodbye.

Friday morning came, and my next-door neighbor, Susan, met me at the foot of her driveway with tears in her eyes. She had agreed to drive me to the airport. I remember moving into the house next door to her and her fiancé. She didn't know it at the time, but my husband and I had walked through the skeleton of her home several times before we met her on our move-in day.

Susan's house was being built at the same time

ours was – though hers was a few weeks farther along in the build timeline. We'd go over to their lot like two kids up to mischief. We'd walk through the construction site – comparing similarities and differences between our home and theirs. We were so excited to be experiencing such a huge milestone.

We had closed on our home on October 31, 2014. Halloween. Susan came over that day to welcome us to the neighborhood. She brought with her an orange pumpkin bucket and some candy as a gift. She'd suspected we hadn't had any time to prep for the neighborhood trick-or-treating considering how busy our day must have been, and she was right. On that day, I gave her the first of what would be many more hugs to come. Susan had the sweetest spirit. I didn't know that our last hug would come so soon and so abruptly.

Together, Susan and I loaded nine suitcases into the back of her small SUV. There was a pregnant silence during our loading. Each piece of luggage felt so much heavier than they probably were in reality. Every single lifting of a suitcase from the pavement felt so symbolic… so final.

When we packed everything in, she looked at me and pulled me close. She gave me the tightest hug. Once again, this was a huge whirlwind of an incident that was put before yet another person in my life. As with the few people before her, she took her role in assisting me very seriously and didn't try to stop me. She, too, believed that I was doing what I needed to for my safety and future. We hugged and climbed into her SUV.

If we talked at all during the ride to the airport, I don't remember it. I don't remember if there was music playing or silence. I don't remember if my eyes were closed or open. I just remember swallowing everything I could. Swallowing emotions, fatigue, heartbreak, and uncertainty. I swallowed everything I could on that ride. I perfected my numbness. I had a plan to execute and was almost on that one-way flight to San Jose, California. I would figure the rest out when I made it. But I just needed to get on that flight with no issues.

We pulled up at the Delta Terminal of the

Charlotte airport. I hopped out of the car and rushed to the back of the SUV. I had to keep moving. No time to feel. No space for it. My neighbor helped me unload the nine suitcases from the trunk. She offered to help me take the suitcases into the airport, but I declined. I did not want to spend another second with a person that I knew. I needed to feel numbness. So that I could continue with a clear head. I struggled to roll all of the luggage into the airport. But I did it.

I went to the counter to check my bags… all nine of them. The Delta representative looked at me like I was crazy.

"Do you know how expensive this is going to be?" she asked.

I put the first suitcase on the weight machine and said, "I'm checking all of them."

She blinked a few times and began the process of checking my bags. After tagging all my bags and adding all the overweight baggage fees, she let me know that I owed $1,300.00. I gave her the cash, then walked to my security checkpoint. It was happening.

As much as I tried to avoid feeling and thinking — I thought about the friends that I had in Charlotte who I would eventually tell that I was no longer living there… and all the coworkers and mentors. I had only told a few close people.

I thought about the years that I had spent loving and growing with my husband. All the chapters that we had planned to step through together. I thought about all the hurt and disappointment that I felt. It was heavy, heavy stuff.

2

ROOTS, OR THE LACK THEREOF

"No forest, just trees. Floating, not free." – Tank and the Bangas,
"Colors Change"

As far as I can remember, my entire life has been fluid. I can't say that I have ever felt grounded in any one particular place. It's hard to explain… but it's my truth. Selling the house in Charlotte was not as hard for me as one might think. I've never felt that I had roots anywhere.

When I was the tender age of one, my mother was tragically murdered. This happened in Atlanta, Georgia, where my mother, father, Corey, and I lived at the time. After my mom's death, Corey and I were sent to Alabama to live with my maternal grandparents.

There were high tensions surrounding my maternal and paternal families, with Corey and I being caught at the center of them. As a result, Corey and I only lived in Alabama for about fourteen months before moving to a small town in South Carolina to be raised by my Aunt Rose on my father's side of the family. My dad remained in Atlanta at that time.

Simply put, living with Aunt Rose in South Carolina was rough. She was not a nurturing woman. She carried a stern demeanor, and it seemed as if she found pleasure in intimidating those around her. My brother and I were no exception.

When I was ten years old, my Aunt Rose evicted

me from her home, ordering "let your dad and Laketa raise you." I can still hear her saying those words in my head today, nearly two decades later. She was angry at the time, but there was finality in that command.

Laketa was my father's fiancée. She and her two children, a boy and a girl, became my new family. They had become family long before the day I moved in with them, though. Our parents had introduced us when I was five years old and Corey was eight. Kee Kee and Jeremy, my new sister and brother, were four and six, respectively.

I was honestly blessed to have such a beautiful new family, though the sting of yet another change in guardianship would leave its wounds. My dad was engaged to be married at the time, but would continue to work in Atlanta for a few more years before taking permanent residence with us in South Carolina.

Laketa never called us her step-kids... and we never referred to one another as step-relatives. Laketa is my mom. Jeremy and Kee Kee are my siblings.

I was a strong, resilient kid – but there was so much disappointment that I carried throughout my circumstance. I felt let down by the people around me who were supposed to love and protect me. Despite me demonstrating the ability to be strong, I wanted to be noticed in all of the chaos. I wanted to be treated like a child who required nurturing, and I wanted it to be freely given. Yet somehow it seemed as though my resiliency and strength served primarily as a convenience for my family members.

I distinctly remember a time shared between my dad and me when I was in high school. He was driving us to the grocery store with just the two of us in the car. In this moment, I felt the overwhelming urge to share my feelings, but did not quite know how to express them. I so badly wanted for some sort of savior but didn't know how to articulate it.

Yes, there was now a home around me. I was surrounded by people, by love. But there was so much hurt packed down inside me, behind the straight As, busy schedule, and resiliency that I seemed to show. I wanted so desperately to be coddled and shielded – but, again, I wanted these things to be freely given. I wanted something from my father that I'm not sure he was aware of… or equipped to give.

I decided to sing a song to my dad that I had written in the sixth or seventh grade. By this time, the song was about four or five years old. My father had moved to South Carolina from Atlanta. My family had moved from the small three-bedroom house we had occupied in Gadsden, South Carolina, to a larger, five-bedroom house in Columbia, South Carolina – or "the city," as we called it.

As we sat in the car, I told my dad that I wanted to sing a song to him that I had written when I was younger. I began singing.

"I'm so confused… feel so used / it's like I'm in this world alone / I can't… sleep at night, tryna find… a way to carry on / Got questions about the way it woulda, coulda, shoulda been / filling my mind, why's this happening / Oh, Lord… give me a sign, a gentle reply / and let me know that you are still by my side

/ and that….

My day is coming, it won't be like this always / I'm one more tear closer… it washes away the pain / I rest assured in knowing that He is there / And He said He wouldn't put more on me… than I can bear."

We had pulled into the BI-LO parking lot by the time I had finished my song, though I don't remember much after that. Once the song was over, I can't recall there being a real response. I don't know if the moment was too emotionally heavy for my father. Or too unsettling to pry into. Too uncomfortable to question. Either way, there weren't many words.

That moment still stands out to me today because it symbolizes the manner in which my father handled the sad and difficult parts of my life… our life. I knew the lack of communication on the issue was not because he didn't care. I knew that he cared about me and loved me very much, but it seemed easier for him to avoid delving into the reason that I felt such gloom and heaviness.

I believe that it was too uncomfortable for him to survey why his daughter would feel inclined to write something so somber yet so sure at such a young age. Maybe there was too much for him to confront, at least out loud. So it seemed that the easiest thing to do was nothing.

I recognized that. Accepted that. Digested that.

Being truly vulnerable in that moment yet having such a lack of response hurt me. It literally hurt me. But I swallowed it. And every other moment that I felt I needed him as my savior. I didn't look to him for reconciliation for the past. He was a person that I couldn't expect to really acknowledge the circumstance I was placed into. Or so I felt at the time. The tumultuous dynamic of my childhood was not something we were naturally going to discuss.

And so, in this moment and others, I continued to build a resolve within myself. Inwardly, I was deeply disappointed at the fact that my dad didn't seem to take more of a vested interest in my well-being. But I perfected the art of "making it." No matter how hurt or under-nurtured I felt, I swallowed it and tried my hardest to never allow people see me affected. I hoped that if I could navigate through life as if it didn't matter, one day it wouldn't. I honestly felt that any frailty of mine would have been an inconvenience to others anyway – with everything else folks seemed to be preoccupied with.

They call it resiliency. I call it self-sufficiency. Survival even. On every level, especially emotionally. My plan was to be tactical and accomplish enough to be fully independent, where I wouldn't need or expect anything from anyone. So that there would be no opportunity for letdown or disappointment.

Once I landed in San Jose, sleeping on my family friend's couch was no more uncomfortable for me than sleeping anywhere else. Having my entire life packed up into nine suitcases just... was. Opening those suitcases up every night to pull out what I needed for a shower, then opening them again in the mornings to take out things I needed to prepare for the day... it just was.

Finding myself there, needing her, was what was hard. That was a position that I despised being in. I had worked so hard to be in a position of self-sufficiency. Just a few weeks prior, I had felt perfectly secure and "put together." The fact that I now found myself desperately needing someone, that I desperately needed that couch, was uncomfortable for me.

I settled in over a few days, before going back to work, this time on the West Coast. My Charlotte-based managing director and I had set up a situation where I could work remotely out of the office space that his peer in San Francisco ran a team out of.

I showed up to the office building in San Francisco as an unscathed, robotic version of myself. I did this on my first day and each day following. I'm still not sure where I packed all that pain, but somehow it had a place to go.

I'd commute between San Jose and San Francisco

for two and a half hours each way, each day for work. I made this work. I had to keep going without showing one glimpse of pain or one remnant from the rupturing of my entire life.

On top of managing the commute and the working hours, I would run for a few hours in the evenings. This was an attempt to continue the marathon training routine that began months before my escape from Charlotte. I had trained for five months before my move to California, and I couldn't bear to see all that hard work go to waste. The marathon was only four months away, so I had to keep going. I didn't want Aaron to take that milestone away from me. I didn't want to stop moving. I didn't want to be still.

This new dynamic was tough, to say the least. After about three weeks of working remotely for my team in Charlotte, I received a call from a team member expressing concern about my connectivity. There were some morning emails that I hadn't been responding to quickly enough.

I remember breaking down on the other end of

the phone, knowing that I was commuting more than two hours in the morning and again in the evenings. Knowing that I would rise at 4:00 a.m. to make it into the office before 7:00 a.m. in effort to avoid inconveniencing my team, given the three-hour time zone difference.

There had been many accommodations made by my team up to that point in support of my relocation, and I appreciated them for being in my corner. Still, when I heard this feedback I remember wanting to scream. I remember wanting to demand, "What could you possibly expect me to do?" I wanted to convey that I barely had time to find an apartment at that point and that I was literally giving everything I had to align with the Charlotte schedule, despite the five-hour commute each day.

I didn't say any of this, however. It had been my decision to move across the country. So my response was that I would fix it.

I could sense that my teammate felt guilty for even mentioning it. He assured me that I didn't need to take any rushed actions on my end, but I responded that my only option to fix the expressed concern would be to immediately secure an apartment that was closer. Even though I was doing my absolute best to operate on the opposite coast in a way that would not pose as a burden to others, I wasn't quite cutting it at the time.

Over the next two days or so, I signed a lease to a new apartment. Up to this point, I'd only had the opportunity to visit about three places in the Bay Area. But my livelihood, my trajectory depended on me making this work until I could find another gig that was local. And so I signed a new lease. I chose what I saw as the best option out of the three complexes I had seen, each having been in three different cities – Oakland, Hercules and Emeryville. Unfortunately, the place that I chose was about forty-five minutes from my job… on a good day. But relative to the commute that I had – it was a third of the time! I signed the lease in Hercules and would be moving in a few days later.

Just like that, I transitioned to my next place in July of 2016. At least I had a place of my own and would be out of my family friend's way, though she never treated me as being in the way at all. Unfortunately, the four weeks I had stayed with my family friend didn't leave me much time to save. With legal fees, moving expenses, and the cost of shipping my car across the country, I had blown through so much liquidity and was beginning to mount in credit card debt.

My maternal grandmother helped me a great deal financially during this transition. She really did have my back. Thanks to Phillip, the Charlotte-based vice president who had helped me before, I learned of an employee crisis relief resource offered by my company as well. The resource team paid the security deposit for my new apartment and covered my first month's rent. I was extremely grateful for all the help.

Back in Charlotte, there was a house to sell. My realtor decided to put the house on the market the Friday following the 4th of July. I received an offer the very same day from a couple that felt that it was the perfect home for them. We were able to close thirty days later.

This worked out perfectly, because the furniture items that had been left in my home to stage for viewing could finally be packed up and shipped to me. My parents, my brother Jeremy, and my little nephew packed my furniture into a shipping pod that I had placed in the driveway of my Charlotte home, and the pod was then shipped to my new residence in Hercules.

I remember the day that my pod arrived at my new home. I was inside my apartment, but I did not feel any more connection to it than I had the couch in San Jose.

Familiar items were being carried in from my old home, but I remember feeling numb. I had been going through the motions that day, mainly checking off moving to-do list items. I was the queen of executing plans. Even at that time, achieving goals (whether day-to-day goals or milestones) gave me a needed sense of accomplishment. These tasks and goals kept me busy. The to-do lists gave me something to look forward to from one minute to the next. Feeling… grieving… were not on the list.

The doorbell rang, and I was shocked to open the door to flowers. I opened the note that accompanied them and learned that they were from my best friend, Monnie. I may have been continuously moving through the day, numb to all that it meant – simply checking it off as another logical thing to do – but not Monnie.

In the letter, she welcomed me to my new home and let me know that she was so very proud of me. I cried. Something I admittedly didn't do enough of in those early days. I stopped moving for the first time that day and leaned against my kitchen counter, allowing tears to flow down my face. It was the closest thing I had to a hug at that time. Surprisingly, I found them to be a bit soothing.

I looked around the now full, box-infested, 600-square-foot apartment and soaked in my new scenery. My new home. Furniture that had traveled 2,700 miles, trailing behind nine suitcases. Suitcases which had trailed behind a twenty-six-year old woman. A woman who had left her husband and love of her life… her career, her friends and mentors, her home, and her well-calculated plans in Charlotte.

I was standing ten toes down in a completely new circumstance, one that had only been in the works for a mere few weeks. At best, I could plan for a few days at a time until I could conceptualize what my new life in the Bay Area would need to look like. This was the new place I was to call home.

3

ANGER & BLISS

"I tried to keep myself busy. I ran around in circles, think I made myself dizzy." – Solange, "Cranes in the Sky"

Grief manifested itself in different stages during the months that followed my separation. Anger was most frequently felt those days, though I did my best to hide it from others. Rage may be a better way to describe it. I was livid, in fact! Livid at the thought of all the possibilities and potential I had let slip through my grasp in an attempt to remain grounded enough for a man who didn't appreciate the weight of my sacrifice. I felt that I had given up so much. So much.

I thought on the potential that I had when I was graduating as the valedictorian of my high school. I thought on the fact that I had been granted an aggregate $1.1 million in scholarships. The fact that I was accepted into thirteen colleges. The fact that I had full-ride scholarship offers from Spelman, Emory, and other universities. I thought about the fact that I could have moved anywhere in the country for college… anywhere in the world. I felt incredibly foolish for deciding to remain in my hometown for college and for not leaving the Carolinas sooner.

I felt stupid for many of the spiritual beliefs I had as well. I had put so much stock in the destiny that I felt was calling Aaron and me. I had believed in the signs and spiritual confirmations that I thought affirmed my calling as his "rib." There had been prophecies given to me during my life that I believed were being fulfilled through our union. I felt like such an idiot for believing all of it.

In this new life I was living, with all the new people I was meeting, how could I possibly explain the experiences that reinforced the decisions I had made as a young adult? How could I, with a straight face, use spiritual convictions as a basis for why I got married at twenty-two years old?

As smart and mature as I thought I had been my entire life up to that point, I suddenly felt so foolish and "country." I felt like a silly small-town girl who had missed out on important experiences during the prime years of her life. Years that could have been spent on exploration, studying abroad, and developing independently. I resented myself for not taking advantage of Ivy League opportunities that would have been available had I just opened my mind beyond the few options conceivable to me as a high school kid. In those days, I hated that I did not know what I did not know. Unexpectedly, I was embarrassed by the decisions I had made.

I was angry with Aaron. I was livid. I had given my life to him. I had packaged all the goodness and love and support and vision and hope and loyalty and purpose that was inside me and joined with him. I had supported him. I had chosen him. I held him down when things were ugly. I was naïve enough to believe him when he said he was remorseful and wanted to try harder.

I was angry with the way that my religious mentors had treated me when they offered counsel. I was angry that my initial urge to leave was chastised. "You are in covenant," they said. "You need to move out of the way and let God heal your marriage," they said. "You need to anoint his head with oil while he's sleeping and pray more," they said. "If he stays out late and comes home angry, you should be meek and patient and pray for him," they said.

I was livid! I felt like I had sold myself short. That I had chosen to reduce myself in so many ways in an effort to be what Aaron needed. What about being free and honest and as big and unafraid as my persona really was?

Anger and self-loathing consumed me and kept me from feeling anything that resembled sadness. Or perhaps the intensity of the emotions that I was willing to absorb masked the reality of my sadness. Maybe I numbed the brokenness that I felt with everything else that I was doing.

Solange's album *A Seat at the Table* dropped in the midst of this season in my life. One song, in particular, read me like a book: "Cranes in the Sky."

In the song, Solange talks about trying to drink away the sting of the pain that she is carrying. She speaks of trying to dance it away. Trying to erase the residue of her hurt by changing her hair.

She speaks of running her credit card bill up... thinking a new dress might make it better. She speaks of keeping herself busy and running around in so many circles, she makes herself dizzy.

I felt every syllable of the song. Every expression.

While I was internally consumed with rage, I countered my anger with nonstop activity. I gave up on the training for the Chicago marathon, but I filled my days and nights with everything else I could.

Parties, happy hours, dating, travel, focus groups, music festivals, you name it. I did not want to be still. I did not want to feel anything that was inside me. I wanted to create my own reality. To force a reality that looked better than the hell and anguish I was trying to escape in my mind and heart.

Momentum served me well. In my new region, there was no shortage of adventure to get into. I was always on the move. I was constantly meeting people. Constantly meeting friends of friends and growing my new circle exponentially. Dating was a breeze for me as well. There was no shortage of intellectual men who were eager to take me out.

I was instantly on the move, and no one could tell how deep my pain truly ran. My best friends, Monnie and Hope, would often tell me that they couldn't understand how I could be so strong, silly, and sharp in the midst of so much chaos and disruption in my life. As much as I loved those women, I honestly didn't know how to let them in. I didn't know how to articulate how damaged I truly was. Instead, I would speak to them every single day – and tell them about all the people I was meeting, all the adventures I'd gone on. All the brilliant and fine brothers I dated.

We'd meet up on various occasions in the months to come – a music festival in Philly that September, a long weekend in the Bay where I hosted them and threw a packed house party in October, an incredible birthday trip to Tahoe with ten of my newly made friends, and the Coachella Music Festival the following spring. They would check on me often, but as much as they laid their eyes on me, they couldn't see that inside I was completely frazzled.

My father would tell me over and over again how I was a "boss" and that he'd never seen anything like it. It seemed I was moving on unfazed. I was more than moving – I was living a vibrant life… on the outside. By the time six months had passed and we were approaching the end of the year, I was catching my dad up on the latest that was happening in my life. I had received a promotion, was bringing in the New Year at a house party with friends (likely my first time not celebrating the New Year in a church service), and I was going to a booze cruise on New Year's

Day.

He chuckled and asked, "When are you going to have a lonely Christmas like everyone else?" Ha! He mentioned that he didn't understand how I rebounded from such a disaster so quickly, but marveled at me. He was happy for me.

Similar to my loved ones, when I would meet people in my first several months of living in the Bay Area, no one knew how deep my pain ran. No one realized I was carrying pain at all. I didn't share that I had left an entire marriage back in Charlotte just a few months prior.

In my interactions with people, I was able to lead with a jovial persona. I quickly engaged with the social community. I joined young professional minority groups, some of which were designed to provide community for new transplants in the Bay Area. Those networks were clutch! They gave me countless opportunities to busy myself and numb my pain. I would show up to day parties and other events alone, but leave with a roster of new contacts.

Every single weekend and various days of the

workweek, I had a laundry list of cool things to take part in. And, boy, did I take part! If there was a move to be made – I was there! I was the life of the party in any room. I could dance anyone off of the dance floor, and I most certainly did! My friends would laugh at the Southern style of my dancing and hyping of others. It was also great having so many sights and places at my fingertips – Ocean Beach, Napa Valley and Sonoma, hiking trails throughout the Bay Area.

Though I would meet new people at the events I attended and make great connections, I was always careful to go to events alone. I would be social while I was there, connect with the people I knew if we happened to be at the same function – but I didn't want to be tethered to a person for the day. While I was social and vibrant, I intentionally sustained a level of detachment and fluidity.

On my commutes to and from events, I remember turning up music from the Sirius radio rap and hip-hop stations loud enough to suffocate my thoughts. Before moving to California, my genres of choice were gospel and neo-soul. After my move, however, I refused to listen to love songs. I refused to listen to gospel. I didn't want to hear anything that would lend me to feeling vulnerable. I needed to feel savage. Boisterous. Numb.

In dating, I took the same approach of being spontaneous and engaging, yet completely detached. I wasn't nervous about dating at all. I leaned all in. I believed that I owed it to myself to explore new interactions and different types of people. To learn myself. Especially after having been attached to the same person for ten years. But I was uninterested in having an intimate connection with anyone.

I would let guys know at the onset that I had no interest in having a relationship or falling in love. I made it clear that if they were to develop feelings, I would be out – that my goal was to be selfish and uninhibited. This always convinced guys to try even harder to woo me – but it never worked.

It never worked, with the exception of one guy. Thaddeus was his name. Thaddeus and I had this chemistry that seemed deeper than deep. I honestly had never felt such a soul tie to a person, and it scared the shit out of me! I remember unraveling with Thaddeus when we first started dating. His eyes were gentle… and sincere. His spirit was nurturing. His arms were protective. He felt like *home*. And I couldn't understand why.

The first time that Thaddeus and I spent time alone, we talked for hours straight. Effortlessly. For some reason, I was completely unguarded with him. Completely bare. I spoke to him honestly about my marriage and the night of the abuse. I spoke with him about my confusion around my entire foundation. How I felt like I was starting to relearn myself all over again. It was strange to be speaking so openly with Thaddeus, but he had time. He was patient. He cared. It was as if he hung on to every single word that left my lips.

After sharing so much, I immediately felt embarrassed. I couldn't believe that I had opened up with someone that quickly. That just wasn't my nature. I'm a guarded woman – even with people that I love very much. I told him how I felt having shared so much, so soon. I felt bare in front of him – though strangely enough, I felt so full and swaddled in that vulnerability.

Thaddeus gave me a gentle smile and told me that he would share a personal story with me about his life if it would make me feel better. He said that it was something that he didn't share with anyone either – not even friends. He asked if that would help.

I gave a shy smile and nodded my head yes. *Who am I right now?* I thought. I felt so delicate...like a flower or something. Sheesh!

Thaddeus shared the story with me, and I hung on every word, just as he had with me. In that moment, I felt that we understood one another on a spiritual level. We were very much the same, in the fact that he was guarded and strong as well. But there was something different about his spirit that calmed me. He was a nurturer. He was security. But he was practically a stranger!

This encounter scared me, because I intended to be detached. I felt that I owed it to myself to be detached. What truly frightened me was the fact that I had already been burned once for believing in superstitions. Logic had told me that soulmates don't exist. New experience had shown me that there were dope, amazing people in any part of the world. There was no such thing as needing to be connected to one specific person to be happy. There wasn't a need to be connected to any person at all for that matter. The feeling for me was alarming, but felt safe at the same time.

Thaddeus and I continued to date, and our surreal connection did not wane. A few months went by while we continued to enjoy beautiful times and increased closeness. Closeness was something I never grew comfortable with. As much as I enjoyed Thaddeus, the eeriness about his familiarity never left me.

The dynamic was eerie because I'd never felt so naked and vulnerable in my entire life, yet I felt completely at ease and protected. This feeling refused to settle well with me, despite how nice the thought of it was. I didn't trust falling for someone so soon after a decade-long relationship. I didn't want to give credibility to emotion and intuition. After what I had just been through, I didn't even trust my own judgment at that point.

I decided to pull away before my feelings could develop any further. I preferred dating dynamics where I could easily compartmentalize the utility I felt from the other person, without having a desire for anything more. I chose not to fall for a person, no matter how great they may have seemed. I wanted to do what was best for me, ultimately protecting myself from pain. I decided to date other people who I didn't feel such an attraction to. This type of space and emotional capacity would be better suited for that time in my life. I was complacent being on an intentional island... hiding in plain sight.

I returned to the numb interactions that I had grown accustomed to. Thrill, excitement – but no real level of intimacy. That felt better for me. Because there was too much pain that existed when I was in a state of feeling.

This hurt Thaddeus, but I felt good that I was forthcoming and honest about the position that I was in. Besides, we had only known one another for a few months, which made me feel justified in my decision.

My plan of keeping my prior life an undisclosed part of my current one in the Bay lasted for about eight months. I had managed to develop relationships with people without sharing that I had experienced domestic violence. I hadn't given any indication that my entire life had been turned upside down after a single night's encounter.

I had packed all of this very deeply… and quite successfully. It was eight months later when I decided to open up about these details in a GroupMe chat with about thirty friends and acquaintances. It was March 2017 at this time, and someone posed the question, "What is the single best decision you have ever made?"

Amongst the various responses that were given, I answered honestly.

"My best decision was leaving my husband after the first time he abused me. He had seen abuse in his life, and I had a mother who had been murdered. While I loved him, I 'loved-me-some-Casey,' and there was no evidence that suggested staying was a good idea. I got on a one-way flight to California, and I never looked back."

No one could believe I'd carried all this without them knowing. They were just as astonished that I left after the first time that he physically abused me. In the vein of that conversation, my desire to help heal and liberate people was more important than my desire to be detached from intimacy. That's honestly who I am. My greatest passion is lifting people higher – inspiring them to tap into the greatness that is inside them and to feel empowered to do anything. To transform their own circumstance.

Until that point, the only parts of myself I had allowed to shine through to my new acquaintances were the fun, vivacious parts of myself. This was my first time revealing a deeper part of myself.

Connection. It's such an interesting phenomenon. Somehow, I innately knew that connection, true connection, would unravel me in some way. It's in large part why I had cut ties with Thaddeus around this same time. While I knew that the benefits of connection were plentiful, it was a force that threatened to unravel the manicured facade I had purposefully developed over the last eight months.

And begin to unravel, I did.

4

THE BREAKDOWN

"These walls I'd perfected left me unprotected…from that emptiness inside." – Eryn Allen Kane, "Fragile"

It was June 2017, a full year since I had arrived in the Bay Area, when I finally broke. To everyone watching, including myself, it seemed to have come out of nowhere. I had done such a great job of moving on. In January 2017, I had accepted a job with the San Francisco-based team I had sat with while working remotely. I was now covering the largest technology firms in the country – which happened to also be some of the largest technology firms in the world. What was more, most of those firms were based a stone's throw away in Silicon Valley.

I continued to be engaged with networks outside the office, now having a solid personal base of so many young professionals in the Bay Area. I had made tons of new friends and was still having a blast every single weekend, having the time of my life. Never stopping to feel. Sure, there were moments of rage that I battled from time to time. Intense rage. But, sadness... missing my old life... missing my husband... there was none of that, none I could sense at least. I never slowed down enough to feel any of that.

In June 2017, I finally broke. Despite all the good that surrounded me. Despite all the amazing adventures I had taken part in. Despite the reputation

I had for being full of life and always on the go. Despite having a life that seemingly reflected the smile I wore on my face, all while hiding the weight of the dark things that I carried internally – I broke.

For the first time, I didn't know how to fake it. I didn't know how to fix it. I couldn't fix it. I was mentally and emotionally broken.

I had started having trouble sleeping a few months prior. On a good night, I would only get about four hours of rest. Being alone became increasingly difficult. Sadness seemed to swallow me whole whenever there was stillness or silence. Numbing my pain with experiences and thrills became less and less effective. After a few months, the fatigue was catching up with me. By May 2017, I was not able to sleep at all most days. I sometimes went whole days without sleeping.

By June, exhaustion set in, and I was no longer able to focus on the fast-paced, highly analytical job responsibilities required by my position. I was no longer able to stop the tears falling from the time my feet left the office building in the evenings to the time

I stepped back into the office the next morning. There were days in which I would lock myself in the single restroom at work and cry until I could pull myself together.

The lack of sleep was wearing on my sanity. After three months of not being able to sleep properly, my fatigue, deep sadness, and emptiness had become unbearable.

It could have been the fact that the yearlong legal separation that was required by state law was finally upon me, signaling the beginning of the divorce process. It could have been the fact that the lawyer I had been working with for the entire year leading up to that point informed me that he could no longer represent me since both my husband and I had moved our permanent residence outside the state of North Carolina.

It could have been the feeling of being alone and having to now figure out the divorce process on my own – suddenly having some level of security stripped away from me. It could have been that, for the first time, I was forced to look at the dissolution of a ten-year connection directly in the face.

It could have been that I was also looking at the death of who I was. An identity that actually existed. A full person and identity that I had tried to forget… as if my prior life didn't matter. As if none of it had meant anything to me. I had been a person with dreams and faith and routine and friends and a life that I absolutely cherished.

Maybe it was all of that.

Here I was a year later, having another one of those walks into my managing director's office. I explained that I had been feeling very off lately and that I believed I simply needed to work from home for a few days. That perhaps I needed to allow myself to mourn without the worry of showing a good face for the office.

His response? He said that those on the team who didn't know what had brought me to the Bay Area – the circumstance and the gravity of the things I had left behind – thought I was smart, hardworking, and crushing it. But for the few who did know, which were he and his boss (who happened to be the manager of both my current MD and my previous one) – they couldn't believe it had taken that long for me to ask for a break. They didn't know how I had kept going for a whole year without needing some time to heal.

He let me know that it was okay for me to take all the time that I needed. He told me that being "whole" was more important than anything else, and he would call HR to see what options there were to make sure that I was taken care of. With tears streaming down my face, I thanked him and walked out of the office building to head home.

As I walked to the bus stop, everything around me began to spin. There was a tightness in my chest, and I felt as if I could hardly breathe. I needed to call someone. I needed to talk to someone, to lean on them. I was so tired. So suffocated. I needed someone right then. I thought through the people that I could call. People that I would have felt comfortable being a complete mess in front of. I opted to call one of my friends I had met when I initially moved to the Bay. Though we had grown close over the past year, emotional intelligence was not his strong suit – so I knew there was a risk that he'd feel completely overwhelmed by my apparently sudden meltdown.

What happened was worse than I imagined. He let me know that he was busy and wouldn't have time to talk until after his dinner plans. Granted, I should have told him that I was in the middle of a street, bawling my eyes out, in the midst of a serious breakdown. Unfortunately, expressing emotional distress is not my forte. There was miscommunication in that moment due to our competing personality types, leaving me utterly frustrated... but still in need.

As I stood there confused and disoriented, I felt so very small in a world that was much bigger than me. I felt that there was nothing I could do to pull myself out of the hole that I was slipping into, though I'd tried my best to run circles around it for as long as I could. As I stood there, I realized that I had gotten exactly what I had planned for. I was all alone... with people around me, but no one in tune enough with me to *see* me. I had no one that I was comfortable enough to call on. No one that I felt comfortable being vulnerable with.

No one except Thaddeus. I pulled out my cell phone and texted him.

Are you available?

He responded immediately.

Yes, do you need me to come to you? Where are you?

I dropped to my knees where I was on the sidewalk; for whatever reason, I felt prompted to just let go. I didn't care who was looking. I didn't care how pathetic I appeared. I wanted to be taken care of. To not have to be strong. To be completely broken and have someone catch me. Thaddeus came to me that day. And I thank God, because the mental illness that I was battling was only advancing. I could not have navigated alone through the storm that was brewing.

The feeling of being "off" that I'd described to my managing director turned out to be brokenness beyond anything I had fathomed. I was very ill. My ability to function deteriorated more rapidly than I could have imagined. My mental state was nearly paralyzing. I wasn't able to fall asleep, yet I was completely exhausted from crying, screaming, and thinking about how horrible my existence felt. Everything about my perception was warped. I honestly felt like there was no use in living. Stepping through life just to have one horrific blow after another felt pointless. I was tired of trying just for the sake of trying. I felt like a hamster on a wheel, trying to stumble through emotions for reasons that were meaningless in the grand scheme of things. I felt the deepest hole in my heart. These were things that I couldn't adequately articulate to my family and closest friends. Trying to explain it all was frustrating and, at times, infuriating. It felt better not to talk to any of them. It was dark. It was very dark.

Once my mental illness was clinically diagnosed, I was granted a short-term medical disability leave. By this time, I had already been going days at a time without being able to fall asleep. The lack of sleep impaired my ability to think critically, perform analytical tasks, or have the energy to interact with other people. But now that I was at home, there were no distractions to fill my day. I fell into the most fragile state I had ever been in. I would cry nonstop, all day long. I would sob and scream and hurt. Oh, my heart was filled with so much pain and emptiness.

I felt as if I were nothing. I felt useless. I was no longer able to be around people without triggering paranoia. I felt they were able to look at me and see what a complete mess I really was. Being around people made my head spin and made me want to shrink… to vanish.

There were days I would attempt to drive to pick up something, medicine from the pharmacy or food, and I would become disoriented in traffic. I couldn't remember where I was going or how to get there. I would pull over to the side of the road and cry – pitying myself. I didn't want to deal with anything I was facing. There were days that I did not feel like living. I felt so tired of trying to piece things together. None of it mattered. I was swallowed inside a darkness that was vaster than anything I could ever climb out of.

It was my psychiatrist who diagnosed me as being chronically depressed and advised that I was also suffering from social anxiety and post-traumatic stress disorder. She let me know that stepping through the battle of mental illness that was ahead of me would be especially difficult for me because I was particularly high-functioning. She said that I was wired to fix things quickly and efficiently and that usually I was able to do so. She said the mere fact that I was able to go as long as I had and to secure so much outward stability during that time was evidence that I was extremely high-functioning. But this situation, she said, was not one that I would be able to fix. It would not be one that I would be able to analyze my way out of.

My psychiatrist told me that I would have to allow my brain time to heal. She could not give me a timeframe on how long the healing would take, but she assured me that the body was able to heal itself.

She said just as a scratch on my arm was able to heal, so was my mind. Just as a broken bone heals in place without my assistance, so would my mind.

What was important, she said, was that I protected my mind – just as I would a scratch on my arm with a bandage or a broken bone with a cast. She said I would need to be sensitive to what my mind needed and to do things that would protect it.

My psychiatrist let me know that the medicine she prescribed me would not cure me, but that it would serve as a buoy, helping me to ride the waves as they came. The medicine wouldn't keep the emotional waves from coming, but they would assist me in weathering them a little better.

While I appreciated my psychiatrist taking care in explaining my circumstance and reassuring me, it sounded to me like this circumstance would cost me my job if I didn't heal quickly. At the same time, I struggled to believe that I could ever get better. I felt so far from the person I knew myself to be, I feared that I would be impaired for the rest of my life.

I felt out of control, which was unfamiliar and uncomfortable for me. My psychiatrist had gathered this about me from my answers to the countless questions she had asked and the information she had taken from the surveys I had completed.

I remember her asking me if I made to-do lists. I

told her that I absolutely did – that I made a to-list every single day, even on the weekends. Doing so gave me a deep sense of satisfaction. My psychiatrist explained that my fixation with to-do lists was my way of exerting control over my life. She said that I did not have control over the events that took place in my childhood, but that writing lists as an adult and executing my own plans gave me a heightened sense of accomplishment, because it signified that I was in control.

That was interesting. Insightful. I could buy that theory. It seemed plausible.

After my diagnosis from my psychiatrist, I tried to pull together the resources that I could to help get me back to normalcy, if that would ever be possible. I needed to set up recurring visits with a therapist – at least twice a week. I needed to start doing yoga – to steady my mind.

I had tried Yin Yoga while in Charlotte, and it had done wonders for centering my mind. I was hopeful that restarting those types of sessions would be helpful in nurturing my mind back to health.

My psychiatrist prescribed me a few different medications to aid my mind in the healing process. One to help me focus. Another to help lift my spirits. Another to help me sleep. Two different sleep medications proved to be ineffective, the second one causing extreme bouts of nausea.

My psychiatrist recommended that I not stay alone. She advised that being alone was not safe or helpful for me as I journeyed through my mental illness. She changed my sleep medication for a third time and advised that I be around someone I was comfortable with. She advised that I go somewhere that I felt safe. Thaddeus had been the only person around me who fit her description. He, for some reason, was home. I had to grow comfortable telling him more and more that I needed him. When I did, he was always there. He was *always* there. It never showed that he was fatigued in being there for me.

The lease to my one-bedroom apartment came to an end in July. Once again, Thaddeus was right there to save me. Thaddeus loaded my things into a U-Haul, placed some things in storage, and was there to guide me through every single day of my illness. He never showed that he was tired, though I'm sure that he was many times. He would make sure that I was taking my medicine… even if he had to fight against my stubbornness. There were times that he stayed home from work so that he could be by my side on days that were especially tough for me. He was that much in tune with me. He cared that much about my well-being – with no strings attached. Freely giving it, because he knew that I needed someone. It was something that I couldn't understand, but so desperately needed.

5

THERAPY

*"And now your chest burns and your back aches from 15 years of
holding the pain. And now you only have yourself to blame if you
continue to live this way." India.Arie, "Get It Together"*

It was during my sixth therapy session in which I
was finally able to register meaning in words that
would undoubtedly change everything. I was sitting
on my therapist's couch, visibly annoyed with the

persistent questions regarding my childhood. Three weeks into my medical leave of absence from work, I was desperate to "heal" so that I could return and save myself any further discredit to my career.

Glen was one of three practitioners I was depending on to help pull me out of the paralyzing inconvenience I was trapped in, but she was dead set on inching along the storyline of my adolescence. It was silly. I thought it should have been clear to her that I was in my current state solely because my husband had abused me.

After showing up twice a week for the past three weeks, it annoyed the life out of me to still be examining my childhood. I mean – couldn't we just jump right into the marriage and get to the root of what caused all this brokenness? Sheesh!

My therapist looked me square in the eye and said, "You may be wondering why I'm spending so much time on your childhood. You may be thinking your childhood has nothing to do with why you're in your current state. Casey, your childhood has everything to do with why you're here. It's the reason you married who you married. It's the reason you reacted to the end of your marriage the way that you did. It's the reason you are who you are today."

She pointed to the temples on each side of her head. "You do a very good job figuring things out up here," she said. "You're excellent at it. You develop tactical plans and execute on them extremely well."

She moved her hands lower. With one hand, she did a circling motion in front of her chest. With the other, she cupped her stomach.

"But you have no idea what's going on in here. You don't. You don't know how to register it. You don't know how to sit with it. You don't know what to name it."

I was speechless. Unguarded. I just sat there, blinking. On the one hand, I did not see the correlation between my past life experiences and the man I chose to marry. If anything, my childhood was simply another example of having people who were supposed to love and protect me do something to the contrary. But nothing truly beyond that. On the other hand, she was right about me not understanding what

I felt. I had no desire to understand it, not when it meant submitting to vulnerability or fragility. Besides, I was so good at being busy and productive, I rarely had a chance to feel.

Hell, if there had been any feelings associated with the abrupt end to my marriage up to this point, I made damn sure I was too distracted to notice them. Or did I? Maybe I was just working tirelessly to mask the intensity of my pain with the isolated sensations I had been choosing to indulge in over the past year.

Nevertheless, her perception of my resistance was spot on. "Touché," I said. "Let's see where this goes." I inhaled deeply.

And so the journey began. I allowed her to carefully parse every detail of my childhood, examining any recollection she deemed significant. We continued to step through this slowly over the course of several months. The experience felt strange, yet oddly cleansing.

I would recount some horrid memory in a matter-of-fact tone and then attempt to move to the next subject. She would stop me to acknowledge that there was pain there… even if I wouldn't.

"Oh, what a terrible thing," she would say.

Or, "That is horrible, Casey. You have every right to feel disappointed about that."

She would do this a lot. Over and over. She never got tired of it.

I didn't know that I needed those responses until she offered them. I didn't know how desperately I needed for someone to see me. I was finally seen.

Many times, I can recall my father telling me, "Well, you didn't tell me you felt anything about that. I would have reacted differently had I known you cared."

But here, this stranger was seeing me. Affirming things I had honestly been waiting my entire life for someone to give a damn about. Without a single prompt, saying, "Casey, that was horrible. No child should have to feel that. No child should have to experience that."

Each time she offered me empathy, it chipped away at the weight of my entire existence.

Glen had been right. I did not know how to register what was inside me. The tension and asphyxiation that I carried consumed me. I had become one with it, enough so that the void inside me had felt normal. I had swallowed so much disappointment and anger and rage and hurt and abandonment, that the weight of it all felt completely normal.

I had succeeded with that weight. I partied with that weight. I smiled with that weight. I would visit my family members with that weight. I had been disappointed again and again… all while carrying that weight.

Glen took her time dissecting my past. The more I talked, the more I emerged. And what I discovered was a hurt, abandoned little girl still inside me… yearning for something.

Four months of these conversations went by. Twice a week. Every week. Truth be told, we never did make it to discussing my marriage or my adult years for that matter. We were still covering ground on my childhood months and months later. There was that much there to uncover.

So much began to click after those months of therapy. There was a reason I chose Aaron. There was a reason why certain attributes from a partner, such as compassion and family values, trumped the need for protection and security.

As Glen had suggested, the things I needed to recognize and reconcile had nothing at all to do with the night of the abuse. That night was my ex-husband's first and last time putting his hands on me. We had enjoyed a beautiful, decade-long relationship with four of those years in matrimony. Therapy revealed to me how the person I chose, the qualities that I fell in love with – and the obligations that I never even thought to look for or prioritize – all stemmed from my childhood.

6

SWEET HOME ALABAMA

"I speak of wondrous, unfamiliar lessons from childhood. Make you remember how to smile good." Chance the Rapper, "Blessings"

Alabama was always the place, the only place, where I could find refuge growing up. The dark reality of my unstable upbringing penetrated the walls of my South Carolina home, rendering it inescapable.

Even after I was ordered to leave her home, my Aunt Rose was still able to come as she pleased with attempts to taunt and diminish me. My dad was present many weekends but spent the majority of his time away in Atlanta during the week. I never complained about it – but it left me feeling a bit unhinged in my own reality. Not fully anchored in any one place. While I eventually lived under the roof of my new mother, who loved me deeply and took the care to continue raising me, I could sense that such an abrupt sharing of a mother was tough at times for my younger sister. While I did have a place to call home, my true refuge was elsewhere.

I remember a time in eighth grade when I, furious over some middle-school drama, was sent to the guidance counselor's office to calm down. She asked me to close my eyes and to imagine myself in my favorite place in the whole wide world. I closed my eyes as colors, silhouettes, and sounds vividly came to mind.

She asked me what I smelled. I inhaled deeply and said, "Fish frying in the kitchen."

She asked what I saw, and I told her that I saw my great-grandmother, who was affectionately referred to as "Big Ma." I could see Big Ma sitting in her recliner, positioned in the corner of the living room, next to a wood-burning fireplace. Big Ma's "spit cup" (which was actually a repurposed Spam can) was placed between her recliner and the fireplace. I'd always keep a good eye on where that spit cup was, so that I would not accidentally knock it over and risk the chance of having to clean anything up.

My guidance counselor asked me how I felt. I smiled and said, "Happy... safe."

The feelings that I experienced in that moment were thick and palpable. I could have gone on and on if my guidance counselor had the time to hear how I felt. As my mind had transported me into Big Ma's house, I felt loved. I felt protected. I felt at home. I felt cherished. I felt like every single day was worth looking forward to... just because it was another day with the people I loved so much. People who loved me unconditionally.

Alabama was the home state of my biological

mother. Growing up, my summer vacations were spent there, as well as any extended holiday break of the school year. I had a slew of cousins, aunts, uncles, etc. there who were all absolutely amazing.

When I would go to Alabama, my first stop would usually be to Big Ma and Big Daddy's house to run in and let them know that Corey and I had arrived. Her and Big Daddy's house sat on a hill… my favorite hill in the whole wide world. Some of my favorite moments from childhood involved staying up late at Big Ma's house, watching television. She'd take two tablespoons and place a mound of peanut butter on each of them. I'd climb into the love seat next to her recliner and curl up with a smile, and then we would lick the peanut butter from our spoons and watch late night shows on the enormous, wood-encased TV that sat on the living room floor.

Corey and I would spend the day at Big Ma's house while our grandparents were at work. During the day, Big Ma would watch her "shows," which consisted of *Matlock*, *In the Heat of the Night*, *Murder She Wrote*, and *Little House on the Prairie*. She would also watch her "stories," or soap operas, which were *As the World Turns, All My Children, General Hospital,* and *Guiding Light.* These were the shows that I loved watching with Big Ma the most. Her reactions to the drama were the best! It's likely why I'm so animated when I'm watching television and movies. Ha!

By the time Big Ma's "stories" came on, it was usually the time of day that Big Daddy would be out and about driving around. This would happen like clockwork, so Corey would leave us in the living room and go into Big Ma and Big Daddy's room, sit in Big Daddy's rocking chair and watch his favorite cartoons. Meanwhile, I stuck by Big Ma's side, cleaving to her every word. I learned how to cook by watching her in the kitchen. To this day, her sweet tea is still unmatched.

I received my first lessons on life and men by listening to her stories. Some of those lessons, I picked up simply by watching her move through life. She was strong. She was steady. She was a healer in our family. The nucleus. But there was a lack there that I've only come to better understand in my adulthood. There was a distance between her and Big Daddy that we'd come to perceive as normalcy. My generation was too young to have witnessed the abuse and infidelity that had taken place in her marriage – but we heard the stories nonetheless. Big Ma and Big Daddy stayed together though, for more than sixty years of marriage.

My maternal grandparents took care of Corey and me when we would visit every summer. At times they would drive all the way to South Carolina to pick us up. At other times, they would meet my father in Augusta or Atlanta to get us. But one thing we could always depend on was being able to return to Alabama every summer, and for that I am so grateful.

By the time I could drive and had my own car and license at sixteen, I would drive all the way from South Carolina to Alabama myself. Even before GPS was being used, I was good to go. I would print out directions from MapQuest and make that five-and-a-half-hour drive just fine.

My grandparents were Seventh-day Adventists, so we would have to turn off the TVs every Friday night at sunset and go to church every Saturday morning. My grandmother didn't believe I should be ruining my hair with relaxers, so she would whip up some mixture that would "strip" the relaxer out of my hair (a concoction made from ingredients including mayonnaise and eggs), and she would use a hot comb to press my hair every Saturday morning before church. While I always dreaded the hot comb process, my grandmother would finish off my hairstyle with the biggest, prettiest ribbons, and I'd quickly get over the last painful forty-five minutes. I felt so pretty, like a little doll.

My grandfather would be thrilled to see us sit in the church pew on Saturday mornings. He was a church elder and would often teach Sabbath school, so he would usually leave for church before we did. On the Saturdays that he had to sit in the pulpit at the front of the church, he would look down at us, beaming with pride.

My grandfather led a teenage church choir for a while when I was really young. "Revelation" was the name of the choir. I would climb into his white truck and attend rehearsals with him during the summers. I'm pretty sure I was the only little kid at Revelation's rehearsals, but I would mosey over to the alto section and try to hold down my note and blend in with the teenagers. I don't think I was as successful fooling them about my age as I'd hoped. My grandfather was tickled pink to see me trying to bellow out the notes, and he would encourage me to keep at it.

My grandfather would push me to continue singing as I grew older.

"Sing one song a day, Casey," he would always tell me.

When I became an actual teenager, he'd often ask if I would sing at the sunset service that was held at the church on Saturday evenings, to close out the Sabbath. Whenever I would agree to do so, he would be so thrilled, letting me practice in front of him as many times as I wanted. People from the church loved to hear me sing as well – my mother sang at that same church as she was growing up, they told me.

My Aunt Christy and Uncle Reggie were in

Alabama, too. They were both younger than my mom; Reggie was the middle child and Christy was the youngest. Christy and Reggie were twelve and sixteen, respectively, when my mom died. They were very much like older siblings who I admired when I was growing up.

I looked up to every single thing that Christy did. She was the coolest diva there was in my eyes. When I was a little girl, I would watch her get dressed in the most fly outfits, put on the highest heels, and then spray herself with a purple bottle of Victoria Secret's Love Spell fragrance.

Christy would always sing as she did things around the house. She had the prettiest voice – still does! I always admired that she could sing so well. Christy kept the sassiest short haircuts, too. Her hairstyles were always on point; it's no wonder I wear a short haircut today.

While I admired my auntie, I knew I was absolutely annoying! I was convinced that we were the same age – eleven years was not that much of an age difference. Christy would get so cute to go out with her best friends, Schevon and Tiffany, and I would always beg to come. Christy would, of course, say no. That was hardly ever the final say, as I would go ask my grandparents, and they would usually force her to let me tag along.

One day, Christy got me good. I had whined my way into being able to go to a wedding and reception with Christy, Schevon, and Tiffany. I believe that Christy was in college by this point, but she would always come home during her summer breaks.

I had the time of my life hanging with Christy and her friends! They were all so cool. I would work to get the timing of my laughs and knee slaps in sync when they were gossiping. Again, I was doing a horrible job of fooling older, cooler humans about my age. Luckily for me, and to Christy's annoyance, her friends thought I was just the cutest thing.

After the reception, Christy wanted to go out and party. She drove us back to the house, and I was so confused. My grandfather happened to be outside watering what I now realize must have been his garden.

Christy asked me to run over to my grandfather to ask if she could borrow his credit card for the night. Ah, that was it! She finally valued my adorable personality and art of persuasion enough to grant me a meaningful role in our fun plans for the night. Good for her!

I agreed to and went running toward the back of the yard where Granddaddy stood watering his plants, garden, or whatever it was in that dirt that I never took the time to notice.

Out of breath, I said, "Christy said can she borrow your credit card tonight."

"My what?" he said.

"Your credit card, Granddaddy. Christy said can she borrow your credit card tonight." I put my hands on my little knees, panting for breath.

My grandfather chuckled. Without even looking at me, and continuing to water his plants, he said, "Christy done got you."

It took me a minute to realize what that meant, but when I did, I went running back down to the driveway. Christy's red, two-door Mazda was gone. She had fooled me, I had to give it to her.

It was Christy's best friend Tiffany who let me move in with her when I fled Charlotte and moved to the Bay Area. I've known her my whole life. She, Christy, and Schevon have all always been big sisters to me.

My Uncle Reggie is a man in my life who I've always loved so much. It was Reggie, along with my dad, who really sparked my love for music at a young age. My dad had great, great taste in music. He would always blare Silk, Blackstreet, 112, Dru Hill, Jodeci, K-Ci and JoJo, and others as we rode in his green Mustang, singing our hearts out.

Reggie, on the other hand, could "sang sang" and would dissect the music, schooling me. I remember Reggie playing this cassette tape of Jamie Foxx, back when I'd only known him as an actor on *The Jamie Foxx show*. He'd play side A and then flip it over to side B, saying, "This is real music Casey." It was real music. Reggie and I would bob our heads, me mostly mimicking his nod and hand gestures. After a while, we'd both be lost in it, eyes closed, just singing, humming, and saying "umph" when a bar dropped that was deep.

Reggie introduced me to neo-soul artists like D'Angelo and Musiq Soulchild. I remember us sitting in the front seat of his Chevy Trailblazer, the two of us fake beatboxing to the beginning of "Just Friends" by Musiq Soulchild. It was real music.

I attribute a lot of my taste in music to Reggie and my dad.

I had so many cousins in Alabama as well! We had the best of times together. Destinee, Bree, Jonathan, Benji, Jay Bird, and Justin. We were tight. I had love. I had a childhood there. I could be completely unguarded and taken care of. Protected. I felt protected.

The love and joy I felt in Alabama were a stark contrast to the cold, judgmental dynamic that existed in Aunt Rose's home back in South Carolina. The home that existed on Walter Lane.

Oh, how happy I am to have made it out of the

street called Walter Lane. The cold dynamics on that dead-end street appear to have broken the spirits of many.

7

WALTER LANE

"Open up to the pain that you feel, and you will reveal the right road to heal... you, yeah." Keyon Harrold, "Wayfaring Traveler"

When my brother and I were children, my Aunt Rose would introduce us using the exact same lead-in every time:

"These are the children I raised after their mother

was brutally murdered when Casey was only eighteen months old. I took them in."

She would rattle off the same rehearsed line every single time we met a new person; it never failed. I especially hated the inaccuracy in this story, which she divulged whenever the opportunity served her. I was sixteen months old when my mother died, not eighteen months. But, more importantly, I never once remember her sitting down with Corey and I to gauge how we were coping with the circumstance she so often shared with complete strangers. I never once remember her surveying whether we were okay emotionally. Whether we were sad. Whether we struggled with the situation. There was nothing of the sort. Yet she could so easily and sympathetically broadcast our "horrific" story whenever a guest came around.

One evening when Corey and I were really young, Aunt Rose took us to a church. I must've been only four or five at the time, but I remember it seeming odd for the three of us to be walking into an empty church, where only the pastor was there waiting for us.

The pastor took Corey and I into a separate room and sat us down while Aunt Rose waited elsewhere. He leaned in front of us, so that his head was level to ours, then proceeded to tell us that we did not have the same mother. My mother, he said, was still alive and had left me when I was a little baby. Corey's mother, he said, was murdered when he was very young.

I became very angry. Again, I was a very young child at the time, but I remember being visibly upset.

"My mother is Wanda Denise Lowe-Diké, and she died when I was one!" I yelled.

My brother was quiet; he kept his composure. I'm not sure what he was thinking. Three years older than me, Corey has a temperament similar to that of my father: soft-spoken and nonconfrontational. You never really know what he is thinking… what he is *feeling*. I, on the other hand, cannot stand to be provoked. That's always been a trigger for me.

Aunt Rose must have heard the commotion, and

she burst into the room.

"What is going on?" she yelled.

"My mother is Wanda Denise Lowe-Diké!" I cried.

The pastor proceeded to tell Aunt Rose what he had told us, and I'm almost sure she called him an idiot.

"Her mother is dead," she fussed. "*His* mother is the one that left!"

That was how the stories of our mothers were disseminated to us. I remember my dad being dissatisfied about Aunt Rose telling us this, but I don't recall him making much of a fuss to her about it. I hardly ever remember him confronting Aunt Rose. That's just the way things were. There was this strange dynamic on that family street of Walter Lane. One that was unhealthy and chilling. I don't know if my father was fearful of Aunt Rose or simply passive in nature, but there was an odd limit to his boldness with her. However, there was always something inside me that refused to bend in the same way.

What may have been a few years later, I remember

speaking with Big Ma about the night that Corey and I were told about having separate mothers. Big Ma sat in her recliner shaking her head over and over as I recounted the events of that night.

Big Ma told me that she was so hurt when she found out that Aunt Rose had told us. There was never a reason for that to be discussed, not while we were so young. She asserted that Corey and I were siblings and that the family loved Corey with all their heart. She was so hurt when she found out what had happened.

Aunt Rose was often bothered by the fact that Corey felt such a closeness to our family in Alabama.

"Poppy is not your real grandmother," she would say to Corey. "She is a witch."

"Poppy" is what we call our maternal grandmother. My mother decided that is what we would call her. We still refer to her as such today.

As previously mentioned, there were tensions that were in play long before Corey and I were old enough to understand any of it – and because of them, Aunt Rose had a serious issue with Corey being close to our family in Alabama.

Aunt Rose had issues with a lot of things, though I still can't quite pinpoint where her general coldness stemmed from. She moved through life in a way that demanded not only respect, but fear. This was true in her interactions with men, women, and children. There was a dominance that she skillfully commanded in whatever environment she stepped into, and that dominance would often stifle any sort of peace, laughter, or comfort we dared to take part in.

This was especially true in her home. Whenever she walked into the house from work, there was a fear that rattled through everyone – my cousins who might have been in our rooms playing… my brother and I… everyone. We would literally stiffen and brace ourselves for whatever she might yell when she came into the home. We never knew what we might have done wrong. Just *being* could be wrong.

Aunt Rose would often refer to me as a "heifer" and find any reason to scorn me, slap me, or otherwise strike me. I honestly believe that she loved to see me flinch. She despised the confidence that she recognized in my eyes. She knew that I could see her. That I had an assured opinion of her. That I would not allow her to break me or my spirit – even if she could physically hurt me.

She openly described me as "fast," a word synonymous with promiscuity in our rural town of Gadsden, South Carolina. She would often berate me for allegedly "looking at men in the gas station," then tell my aunts and uncles falsehoods of me doing so. I would hear her tell fabricated stories about her catching me pulling up my shirt to "flash" my older male cousin. I was a young girl at the time, yet she continued to spread these damaging and disgusting lies. Underneath the toxicity and hatred, I knew that her tactics were intentional. A sick method of bringing folks into subjugation.

I refused to let her break me. No matter what the tactic of the day was, I would look her in the eyes, fearless and strong. Despite her beatings and her name-calling attempts to corrupt my psyche, I never broke. I never shrank. I knew that I was strong enough to outlast this hell. That I would survive it and move on. That this wouldn't be permanent for me.

My interactions with Aunt Rose did not cease after I was forced to move out of her home. My family and I continued to invite her to events and functions, as was customary in our Southern tradition. I remember a painful day in high school in which she attended the senior citizens breakfast I had invited her to. My high school hosted this event for students to bring elder members of their families.

I noticed she had in her arm a manila folder, but I thought nothing of it. I sat and talked with her, doing all that I could to have a pleasant interaction throughout the function.

Suddenly, during a poem reading, she opened the folder and leaned close to my ear.

"Have you seen this before?"

I looked down and saw newspaper clippings.

Headlines reading "Woman Murdered." The newspaper clippings had pictures of a man; I can't remember if he was in a courtroom or posing for a mug shot. Maybe it was both. It was clear that this was an exposé of my mom's murderer, which was being thrust on me at a family breakfast in my high school cafeteria.

There were a number of clippings that she continued to flip through while sitting beside me.

My head and heart were pounding. *How dare she? How dare she do this to me?* I thought.

I didn't really start asking questions of my own about my mother until after high school. Up until that point, I couldn't bear to. Surely, she should have known I didn't want to see these clippings during a poem reading in the middle of a public ceremony.

Outwardly, I showed no reaction. I resorted to my typical response to her antics: dormant, yet present after all these years.

I clinched all my hurt, sadness, and anger back with my teeth and swallowed very, very hard.

"No, I haven't seen those," I said and gazed forward.

She tilted her head to the side.

"You haven't? You sure? You seem like you've seen them before."

In my head, I'm thinking: *I seem like I have seen them? What does that even mean? Because I didn't give you the troubled reaction you were looking for, you're puzzled?*

I couldn't believe her. At that point, I just wanted to escape. It took everything in me to hold it together.

When we moved to the tables to eat breakfast, she showed at least one other person the newspaper clippings – leading off with her usual line, "Her mother was brutally murdered when she was eighteen months old.... I stepped in to raise her and her brother... yada yada yada...." It was the same old story of heroism. I was absolutely out of it by then. A shell. Just trying to make it through to the end to end my misery.

Once I arrived back to my classroom, I completely broke down. Sobbing. Hurt by what I saw. Hurt by the fact that she would do that to me and remain so cold. Hurt that life was so unsettling and that had to be so strong in spite of it all.

Looking back on it, I suppose I didn't have to be strong. It was somehow just in me to be so. I could have easily folded. I could have broken down when she first opened the folder, as she had expected me to, but my spirit forbade me. That spirit likely being the very thing that prompted years of her mistreatment towards me.

There was a moment when I attempted to speak candidly with Aunt Rose about the pain of my childhood, to have a dialogue about it. To open myself up and tell her that I was hurting.

I was in the first semester of my freshman year of college, living in a single-style dorm with no roommate. It was my first time really occupying space alone, and in the newness of my collegiate environment, I hadn't yet piled on activities to fill my time and mind. In this newfound stillness, sadness overwhelmed me. My mind was flooding with memories of my childhood, memories that made me cry and feel a bit paralyzed.

One day, I called Aunt Rose on my cell and let her know that I would like to come down and talk to her.

On the other end of the phone, she asked, "Well, you're not pregnant, are *you*?" Her tone was almost hopeful. I shook my head and kept my composure.

"No, I'm not pregnant, Aunt Rose. I'm not having sex. I would just like to come and speak with you about something that is serious to me."

She said that she would be looking out for me to come. Not even an hour later, my dad called to let me know that Aunt Rose had called him, asking if I was pregnant. I can't say that I was surprised. I sighed and confessed that I wanted to go down to confront Aunt Rose about the horrible childhood that I experienced with her. I explained that her first reaction was to ask if I was pregnant and that she probably wished that I was. I only wanted to go and speak with her face to face.

I made it down to Aunt Rose's house, and I went

for it. Tears started streaming down my face, but I went for it.

"I want to talk with you about my childhood. There are things that really bother me. It makes me really sad all of a sudden, and I'm trying to find a way to deal with them. When I was in the fifth grade, you kicked me out of your house – "

"I sure did!"

Man, that hurt. Man… that hurt. I stiffened up a little and stopped crying. I proceeded to let her know that it was hurtful when she would constantly introduce me as the child whose mother was brutally murdered. I told her that doing this was especially damaging because she never sat down to talk with Corey and I to see how we were coping from such a traumatic life start.

She responded by scoffing and saying that I was too young to have even been thinking like that. She insisted that I would have never put that much thought into any of those things a child.

The conversation was fruitless. My being

vulnerable in that moment was fruitless. I continued a toxic relationship with Aunt Rose throughout my life because that seemed to be the only option I had. It seemed to be the only choice to make.

At least I had made it away from her close reach – no matter the consequences. That was a relief in itself. I was now in college and didn't have to depend on her for anything. Even still, I wonder why my father never truly defended me… in these instances or any others that I would share about Aunt Rose.

Was this why I married someone who didn't have a protective bone in his body? Is this why a sense of security was never something I knew to prioritize? These are things I didn't know to question until after the depression had struck. Until my therapist forced me to look at the painful memories of my past – session after session, until I finally relented.

I distinctly remember calling my father from Alabama one summer when I was in elementary school. I asked him to allow me to move in with my maternal grandparents in Alabama. I assured him that they would take good care of me. That they would put me into a good school. That I could not stand to live with Aunt Rose in South Carolina any longer. I begged him. It was my first time breaking down and asking for a way out of my misery.

He said no. He said that he couldn't let them win. I don't know if he meant to say that aloud to me – a kid who was bearing much more than anyone probably realized. But he said it. I remember.

He said, "I can't let them win." And so, there it was. I would have to return to South Carolina at the end of the summer.

I didn't last much longer living under Aunt Rose's roof. It was during the school year following that summer vacation when she kicked me out. I wonder what my dad thought then. I wonder if he ever thought back to the day that I begged him to allow me to move. The day that I told him that things were bad in the home with Aunt Rose.

I wonder what he thought about the situation. His daughter being kicked out of her home in South Carolina, while he lived in Atlanta, Georgia. I wonder if he had shared with Aunt Rose that I had asked to leave, and if that was the catalyst behind such an irrational decision. Whatever the case, I never remember my father and I talking about it.

I never felt protected. I was exposed to the world. And I had to figure out how to become immune. I had to figure out how to shield my vulnerabilities. How to become impenetrable. Because Alabama was too far away to be my refuge. The people that loved me unconditionally were too far away to protect me day-in and day-out. I was exposed… and so, with my will and my resolve, I built this shield.

I would become accustomed to moving on without looking back. Befriending people, but never really letting them get close enough to hurt me. Wearing strength and a smile, no matter how badly I was bruised internally. Working hard and excelling at everything imaginable, because that would be my ticket out of my circumstance.

In fairness, I wonder if that had become the coping mechanism of those who were a product of Walter Lane. For my father and for my Aunt Rose, who had grown up on that same land before him. I wonder if all three of us had been raised by parents who had not received the warm embrace and kindness each of us so desperately needed and desired. A reality that had caused each of us to become somewhat detached – as a way of protection. A mechanism and toughness that my Aunt Rose learned in her childhood and my father in his as a means of survival. One that had allowed me to press on and do what I had to do… to wear a toughness and maintain a distance that seemingly kept me safe from any level of hurt.

Maybe we were all suffering from the same hurt… from the same lack. Maybe all three of us were simply doing the best we knew how.

8

DÉJÀ VU

"Been doing my best to move on, but the pain just keeps singing me songs." India.Arie, "This Too Shall Pass"

Therapy had encouraged me to start talking about things that I never really allowed myself to speak to. I was being asked pointed questions about my life and my feelings. I was able to speak freely without the need to tailor my response as to not cast blame or judgment on the family members that I loved so much. Therapy unpacked so much that I had internalized, things that I had no desire to stuff back down once they were exposed.

Glen's continued validation awakened something in me. It offered me solidarity and affirmed that I had every right to feel disappointed and bruised. It made me realize that a child should have been protected, no matter how resilient and unaffected they appeared to be. Glen made it clear that my pain should not have served as an inconvenience to the adults around me, who seemingly had bigger fish to fry. She helped me to see that I didn't have to be as strong as I'd been conditioned to be my entire life.

For the first time, I wanted to understand the complexities of my childhood. I wanted to understand why my environment had been so tense. Sure, things were more stable once my father moved to South Carolina and we were all under one roof. He had done a fantastic job putting me into camps and leadership academies that would hone my skills and intellect. He was around to challenge my mind and took pride in seeing me grow. I loved my father more than anything else in life, and none of my disappointment stifled that.

But there were so many things that had taken place before he moved under the same roof with me... things that had impacted the way in which I carried myself as a woman. At twenty-seven, I was finally ready to ask questions about the circumstance I was born into. To better understand the tension and bitterness that surrounded me when I was growing up.

I decided to no longer hold off on asking these questions for the sake of avoiding discomfort. This was a part of my life, too. These factors affected me, too. I, too, was carrying deep, deep scars from the horrible events that took my mother away. I wanted to better understand the dynamics that surrounded my childhood.

In mid-August of 2017, I finally began asking questions of my father and Poppy. I asked precisely why Corey and I had been taken from my grandparents' home in Alabama to live with Aunt Rose in South Carolina. I had always heard stories of events that followed my mom's death. Stories of why things were tense between my paternal and maternal families. But I had left the stories at that: as stories. I'd never asked the explicit question: "What happened?"

I already had pieces of the story, as told through my Poppy's eyes. I had heard how she gave us up so that she could live to be around to support us. Her doctor told her that her blood pressure was dangerously high, likely elevated from the loss of her eldest daughter. It was his opinion that with the tensions and drama that existed between her and my father's family, she wouldn't live to witness me turn eight years old.

Her doctor advised her that she had to find a way to lower her blood pressure. And so... she let Corey and I go. She gave us up so that she could live to be there for us through the long run. She did it because she knew we were going to need her. That's the way Poppy would recount the events to us. Not that we would ask – but so that we would know.

In the thick of my depression, I was determined to seek answers on my own. I wanted to be able to understand the decision for myself... the actual events that led to us leaving.

The truth pained me, sending shivers down my body. The events that led to the permanent farewell for Corey and I seemed as swift as my Aunt Rose's act of kicking me out of her home seven years later.

Aunt Rose had come to Alabama to visit my brother and me. She had gone to Big Ma's house and asked that we be brought there to see her. It was no secret that my Aunt Rose and Poppy did not get along. Even this battle of how and where Aunt Rose could visit Corey and me was full of contention.

There was some back and forth around the matter, and Poppy decided that she was not going to argue with my dad and Aunt Rose any longer.

That day, my grandfather gave my father a call in Atlanta, saying, "Ann said to come get the kids."

My dad drove to Alabama from Atlanta, arriving

about an hour and a half later. Our things were already packed up in large black Hefty bags, ready to be taken. My grandfather was in the yard when my dad arrived, hurt by what was about to happen. So hurt that he couldn't bring himself to come into the house.

It was said that I lit up when I saw my dad. I was always happy to see my daddy. I loved my daddy so much. And I still do.

On this very day, my dad picked us up and took us to live with Aunt Rose in South Carolina. Just like that. That was it. That's how it happened. It was a decision made that day: abrupt, but final. A decision that impacted the entire life trajectory of my young brother and me.

Like I said, I had heard stories about that day. Bits and pieces through the lenses of various family members in Alabama.

Some said that it felt as if my mom had died all over again when we were sent to South Carolina. Having us there… having my face that looked so much like my mother's, had been somewhat of a consolation. But us leaving the family so suddenly... it was much too hard for my family in Alabama to bear.

My Big Ma would tell me that the family hated what happened that day. That it took a lot for them to forgive the decision to give us up to Aunt Rose.

She told me that when my mother was alive, she would say that if anything ever happened to her, she never wanted Corey and I to be raised by my Aunt Rose. I had heard the same sentiment from other family members as well. My Aunt Rose had been Corey's guardian for a while before my mom and dad were married. My mom didn't want that again for Corey and me. She didn't even want me to spend a single night with Aunt Rose if she wasn't there. She wanted to protect me from her.

I could not help but feel a sharp sting in my chest. The severity of the moment and finality of the decision reminded me so much of the anger that drove my Aunt Rose to tell me to let my dad and Laketa raise me.

It was too reminiscent of the way that I was

handed off to someone else years later. While I knew that my Poppy loved me and contributed so much to my entire life, the sting of her actions clung to my chest.

Poppy called the next day, regretful, asking for us to come back, but the decision had been made.

It stung me so much that adults could be so rash about matters that affected children. How they could be so lost in bickering, so determined at having the upper hand, that the security and sanity of little children were sacrificed as collateral damage.

I know that this was not their intention. I'm absolutely certain that my grandmother would never try to hurt me. But I also knew that my circumstance and the pain I experienced as a direct result of their decisions mattered very much. I knew that my feelings were just as true and present as the tough arrangements that were made by the people that I loved, even if those feelings weren't considered.

Around this same time, I told my father how I remember telling him how bad things were living with Aunt Rose. How mean she was. How I felt like it wouldn't be a good situation for me to keep living in.

I reminded him of my wish to move to Alabama to live with my maternal grandparents. How I tried to assure him that I would be provided for. How I knew that I would be kept safe from Aunt Rose and her mental abuse. Her harsh, merciless hands.

I told my father that he had muttered, "No… I can't let them win."

I told him how defeated that made me feel. And how disappointing it was to have my feelings disregarded. That I was, once again, lost in the debris of a feud that I never fully understood.

My dad's tone got really soft. I could feel his sadness for me. His sadness for us, even. He told me that he probably did say that and that he was sorry that it made me feel that way.

On the other end of the phone, I cried. Still in the thick of my depression, I cried. At that time, I still wasn't ready to tell him that I never remembered him fighting for me. That I never remembered him standing up for me. Protecting me. Rebuking Aunt

Rose for being so ugly to me.

I ended our conversation, harboring even more hurt and resentment, angry that these things were allowed to happen to me. Things that I had no choice but to live with.

9

DEPRESSION

"This is the part that the thugs skip." – J. Cole, "G.O.M.D."

I was sitting inside a restaurant on Haight Street in San Francisco, completely surrounded and crying profusely. I couldn't help myself. I couldn't get out of my head. I couldn't find a way to crawl out of my heart. Up until then I had been successful at packing down pain, but I was now acquainted with depression and along with it an outward display of hopelessness that I could no longer control.

Depression had defeated me. It was more paralyzing than anything I could have ever imagined. It was almost as if I was watching myself from the outside – going along for whatever gut-wrenching ride my mind or soul decided to take me on at any given moment.

I was empty and full at the same time. There was no more space for me to hold onto anything meaningful. Every painful thing inside me seemed to be vomiting up… yet the need to purge felt constant. Every second of every day. The anguish inside me seemed to be without end.

"You're going to get through this, Casey."

I looked up and remembered where I was. I remembered what capacity I was supposed to be operating in. I remembered how normal I had programmed myself to be… at least for a few hours.

Drew, a good friend of mine from high school,

had come into town to visit his old college roommate. He knew that I was in the area and wanted to see me as well.

Drew and I had actually reconnected some time before my move to California. About a year before my marriage ended, Drew had moved to Charlotte. I'd see Drew fairly often over the course of that year: barbeques at my house, soirees on the rooftop of his place, food festivals in Uptown where we would talk for hours on end about our dreams, obstacles we have hurdled, and the town we left back home.

As it had been with virtually all my friends back in Charlotte, one day Drew looked up and I wasn't there. My number had changed, my social media had disappeared, there were no cars in my driveway. Aaron and I had vanished with no warning. No word of goodbye.

I so wanted to experience this moment as a whole person. I wanted to catch up with Drew after such an abrupt disconnect and hear how things had turned out for him. I wanted to show him how great things had been for me in my new location.

Things *had* been great. I had been living a wonderful life. I had started over. I'd gotten a new number and reconnected with my friends from Charlotte. They were so hurt by the events that took place between Aaron and me, yet so proud of me for taking control of my life.

I wanted to be that person who was still in control. That version of Casey that everyone was so accustomed to seeing, no matter how difficult the terrain was.

The version of Casey that was sitting in that chair was in no state to play host. It had been months since I had been able to interact with friends... for any notable length of time anyway. Any time that I had tried to see friends, tears would ultimately start pouring out of nowhere. The very presence of people who knew me gave me anxiety. It was draining trying to carry on a simple conversation. Trying to focus on the things that they cared about. Trying to hold my breath between every response so that I wouldn't let out the screams and yells that were dancing in my throat.

Interactions with people would always end the same way. While everyone around me was able to laugh, interact, and flow from one sentence to the next – the activity was dizzying for me. I would feel overwhelmed by everyone's eyes on me, fearing that they would notice how off-balance I was and then demand an explanation. An explanation that I couldn't give. I was fearful they would see how distant I had become and wonder why I didn't have anything at all to add to the conversation, why I barely ever came around anymore. A gesture as simple as a smile from a person would sadden me. It suggested a person expected a level of closeness that I couldn't stomach or return.

I would begin to shrink in these situations, wanting nothing more than to disappear. I would finally begin crying in the middle of a conversation, leaving abruptly. Afterward, I would feel so drained that I would lay balled up on the couch for days. Not wanting to risk seeing another person. Not wanting to answer their text messages or calls to inquire what had happened to me. Not wanting to have to explain why I was so *off*.

I so wanted this time to be different. This was only my fourth time attempting to be around a friend since I'd been diagnosed with depression. Since my mental state had received a name. I wanted this time to be different.

Drew and I went way back. This should have been yet another time for us to delve into all the newness that had unfolded in our lives. All the mountains that we had climbed. All the bullshit we had managed to shake off.

I so wanted to be part of making his first visit to California incredible. I so wanted to feel like my normal self again. To be sociable and fun. Instead, I was at the other end of the table, lost in my head and drowning in my tears. It was happening again.

We had started in a large booth alongside two others – his college roommate and another friend he had made the trip to California with. As the three of them talked at the table, Drew saw me withdrawing. He saw my body contracting and my eyes closing for very long periods of time. He saw that I was not well.

Drew stood up from the table and reached out his

hand to me. I didn't know whether to feel embarrassment or relief, but before I knew it, tears were flooding down my face, and so I took Drew's hand. Drew led me to a smaller, private table.

As we sat across from one another, Drew was silent. He allowed me to cry, not asking what was wrong. Not asking for me to explain this all-consuming illness that I just couldn't shake. After some time, the silence broke.

"You're going to get through this, Casey. I know you don't see it now, but you will."

"I won't, Drew. I will not. I will never be the same."

It was my first time saying such a thing. With all the shit that I had been through. All the hurt. All the loss. All the disappointment. I had never, ever felt like I would not make it past an unfortunate circumstance. *Ever.*

Until then, I had always had a plan. I would wiggle my way out of everything. If all else failed, my faith would carry me during the times that I couldn't find an exit. But even then, I was always sure that I would make it through. That I would be okay. I had never given up on anything.

But not this time. I was broken down to nothing. I didn't recognize anything about myself and was seemingly disconnected from every single good thing that I could remember. I was nothing.

"Casey, you will make it to the other side. It's going to happen. I promise you."

I looked at Drew, too tired to repeat myself. There was a pleading in his eyes. He had never seen me so defeated. If he could have taken some of the pain away from me, I know that he would have. He wanted me to believe in my ability to mend. To find strength again. He wanted me to know that it wasn't over.

"Not this time, Drew."

I kept going to my therapy sessions. Twice a week, every week. After a while, I began looking forward to them. Not because they made me feel better. On the contrary, as low as I would feel at times, I would soon learn that there was even more depth to my hurt.

I think that I looked forward to therapy because I found that there was so much for me to unpack. There had been so many memories and feelings that I had kept tucked away for years, decades even. There were so many disappointments that I had been unknowingly carrying with me. From year to year. From state to state. From family visit to family visit. This weight rested behind every smile and every "I love you." This longing and absence grew in intensity, no matter how many times I fixed my own issues.

I became so very grateful for the space to air it all out. Not worrying about what family member I might offend. Not concerning myself with loved ones I needed to protect. Giving air and space to the weight that I had chosen to carry alone, thinking that I was somehow more equipped to balance those pains than the ones who should have shouldered them *with* me.

I realized that I had made it easy for people to disregard my needs. I had fought against the notion of fragility, yet my entire life I was waiting for someone to *save* me. To protect me. To shield me and love me unconditionally. By being so inexplicably strong, I had made it easier for my father to sit back and let life happen to me without playing a more active role in my security and development.

Because he had been so distant and uninvolved, I had viewed my need and longing as an inconvenience. And so the cycle never stopped. No matter what happened, I was onstage to fight another battle – alone. My father had a front row seat and commented on my dynamic performance but didn't put any skin in the game. I tried to swallow this as normalcy.

There was so much to unpack, and therapy seemed to have room for it all. The walls never gave way under the memories that I would recount session after session. The couch never broke under the weight of my existence – whether I sat Indian style, upright, or leaning. The tissue box never ran out of pillows for my tears.

During several sessions, Thaddeus's name would emerge. My therapist became very intrigued in the role that he was playing in my life at that time, as was

I. While I couldn't fall asleep most days when I was living alone, there was a sense of peace and security that Thaddeus brought me. I could rest in his presence. It would happen without fail. There was something soothing about his spirit and role in my life. Something protective.

It occurred to me that the feeling of security that I had with Thaddeus was something that I had never experienced from my father or any other man for that matter. I didn't know to look for it explicitly. I didn't know to value it – yet it was one of the most beautiful feelings in the entire world.

8/2/2017:

Sometimes it seemed that I was getting all the hugs I needed over my lifetime from that man.
Making up for lost time.
Shedding tears that should have been cried long ago, on his chest.
He'd wipe them. With his protective hands.
He'd wipe away the saltiness with his skin.
As if he cared. As if he cared about my pain.

My well-being.

And I couldn't fully understand why he did.

So afraid to trust – afraid of further brokenness.

But in so much need of a kind heart.

A steady shoulder.

He was there for some reason.

Sometimes it seemed that I was getting all the hugs I needed over my lifetime from that man.

My body and mind were so damn tired. I was weak, weaker than I had ever been. Having a source of comfort and protection in my life – even if it was by way of someone I had known for less than a year – felt like *home.*

That's honestly the only word that I have for it. I felt completely safe being unraveled and broken in the presence of Thaddeus. And I knew that he would take care of me, without me even having to ask. I knew that he would move heaven and earth to see me okay. I *knew* this.

Over time, I did heal. After about three and a half

months of being on medical leave, I began to recognize familiar traits of myself. They were hints of my old self in the smallest of things. Things like occasional optimism. Or chuckling again. I finally started having genuine hope that I would make it to the other side of my circumstance.

This time, I had learned a different way out. I learned how to care for myself, rather than averting the crisis. I learned to be patient with my process, rather than rushing to show the best version of myself so that others were convinced that I was unscathed. I learned fragility was part of being human, that it was okay to cry out in pain… to need someone to help me bridge over hard times.

I learned that the mind does heal, just as my psychiatrist had said it was capable of doing. The body is powerful. But so is love. So is fragility. So is pain.

Once I realized I was on a sure way to recovery, I did what Casey would do. I immediately went on a search for my own place, wanting to quickly regain my sense of independence. I didn't want to depend on Thaddeus's if I didn't need to. It was important to stand on my own two feet again, to begin strengthening my legs. Thankfully, I had not been defeated. The old version of myself, the good parts of me, hadn't been destroyed in my battle with depression. I wanted to set back on my quest to climb and lead and inspire. I wanted to have the freedom to continue learning about myself and who I had become.

I was extremely grateful for the nurturing and shelter that Thaddeus had provided me. I always will be. I don't know that I would have recovered in the timeframe or in the way that I did had it not been for his assistance. Now that the goal of seeing me to the other side was seeming to take shape, I let Thaddeus know that I was leaving.

"Are you sure you're ready, Casey?"

"I'm sure. I want to stand on my own two feet. I can. I'm in here again. I can feel it. I want to get back to living."

Thaddeus knew how determined and stubborn I

was. He smirked.

"Yes, she's back."

After about a week of searching, I found the perfect transitional spot. A friend of mine had purchased a home in Walnut Creek and was looking to sublet his apartment in Oakland as soon as possible. I agreed to take over the lease and was told that I could move in as soon as possible.

That was it – I was moving to Oakland. I hired movers to clean out the storage that much of my furniture had been in, and those same movers came to Thaddeus's house to move the rest of my things. In one clean swoop, I was out. On my own again. Preparing to step back into my prior routines – not knowing exactly what to expect, but ready to step back into my life, head on.

10

THE INFLECTION POINT

"This pain don't contain political correctness. I let it pour out however it come." Maimouna Youssef, "Work in Progress"

After four months of being out on medical leave, I returned to work feeling like my full self again. I thought I was there. I thought that the "closure" business had been properly taken care of. My wounds had been tended to. I now had a better understanding of myself and who I was. It was October 31, 2017, when I stepped back into the office, the first day returning to my normal routines and interactions.

Two weeks before I came back into the office physically, my work system access was restored, and I was allowed to start getting reacclimated remotely. Of all the tasks that I needed to do to transition back into my role, the first order of business that I set out was reconnecting with a group of women whom I had been in a networking "pod" with for several months before I took my leave of absence.

"Power of 10," the group was called. It was designed to provide a close-knit circle of trust among women in the workplace. We were to aid one another in succeeding and navigating difficult terrains in the corporate environment. Much as I had done with my close circle in Charlotte a year and a half prior, I had abruptly left this circle of support when my life shattered.

Without explanation or warning, I fell away from the group for an extended period of time. This time, I wanted my resurfacing to be different, especially in the office. I wanted to break my silence around the circumstances that had caused me to step away. I now understood that experiences of trauma and mental illness were very much relevant to dynamics that affect our careers and the attainment of success.

As resilient as I still aimed to be, I had come to learn that suffocating one's frailty for the sake of perceived perfection in the office was not a healthy solution. I realized that tragedy can, and often does, affect everyone – and no amount of planning, hard work, or commitment to excellence can prepare you for its occurrence.

At a grassroots level, I desired to shift culture. To speak aloud about uncomfortable experiences in an effort to kill stigma, in hopes that my encouragement would empower someone else to speak up should they ever need help.

I emailed my Power of 10 group, letting them know that I had taken a step back to mend the mental illness I had been struggling with. I revealed that I had been a victim of domestic violence and that it had turned my entire world upside down. That my life had never been the same since.

I told them that I had suffered in silence for an entire year because I was worried about what the stigma of frailty might do to my trajectory. Contrary to my fears, I found that our company had resources and a willingness to help us when we need it most.

Just as my managing director had once told me, I let the women know that their being whole was what mattered most and that they should absolutely do what they needed to in order to achieve their own wholeness.

After sending the email to my Power of 10 group, I forwarded it along to the managing director of my current group, my previous managing director in Charlotte, and their boss — all the men who had assisted me in my transition to safety and recovery. I thanked them for making it possible for me to even be able to send such a message to a group of women. I thanked them for their role in my recovery.

The day that I walked back into the office, the welcome that I received was extremely warm. There was a huge welcome poster draped across my desk, with heartfelt notes from every single person on the team.

I even received a direct call from the head of our entire business organization, welcoming me back and thanking me for reaching out to women and breaking my silence in an effort to help others. He was extremely moved by my story and admirable of the strength that it took me to endure everything that I had – for myself and now for others.

"You almost got me," he said. "I was honestly choked up. If something were to ever happen to my sixteen-year-old daughter or my wife, for that matter, I would hope that their companies would step in to help them if they needed it."

This was the stuff that mattered to me this go-around – not just on the job, but in life. My impact needed to be fuller and reach more deeply. My honesty needed to show up in all settings. It mattered. Lives depended on it, mine included.

The welcome back was joyous. It felt great to be present professionally. It felt great to be back to my normal routine, with my mind intact.

But it turned out there was a certain routine I couldn't quite return to. I couldn't return to speaking with my father each day as if he played no part in the pain I had uncovered.

He had watched me go from leaving Charlotte to rebuilding in San Francisco to suffering through depression to reemerging back in corporate America as a spectator. Having a front row seat, but never participating as a cast member in this story. But he was just as woven into the storyline as I was. Much more so than my ex-husband or any other man in my life.

It was one night in November when I finally relayed the way that I felt to him. What started as a normal conversation turned into anger and then escalated to rage.

I remember shouting. Crying. Shaking. Being

furious! Having laid out my life and pain for the consumption of my therapist and being affirmed, even validated in that pain… changed something for me.

It meant that I wasn't being overly sensitive. I wasn't being a villain or disloyal by acknowledging that my dad didn't do enough. That he didn't protect me. That he didn't bleed for me. That he hadn't inconvenienced himself once throughout my ordeal over the last eighteen months.

Not surprisingly, when I laid out my frustrations, my dad hit me with, "Well what did you want me to do? I mean, had you asked me to do something specific you know I would have. You handled the move from Charlotte to San Francisco so well I didn't know you really cared about it that much."

I didn't accept his response this time. Though I expected my father's reaction, I allowed myself to feel – without disregarding it. I was furious that this was my dad's thought process. Furious!

I told him how I felt about everything. Him not raising me. Him stating that he didn't want to "let them win" when I asked him if I could move to Alabama. Him not coming to my defense when Aunt Rose kicked me out of her house in the fifth grade. Him not helping me after I had been abused and fled from Charlotte to San Francisco. Him finally asking how he could help a whole two months after I had moved away. Me letting him know that he could help by packing my household items into a shipping pod – and him telling me the total amount I owed him for the boxes and bubble wrap he had purchased for the packing.

He responded, "Well if you were on hard times, you could have told me, and I wouldn't have asked for the money back."

I was so angry!

We didn't talk for some time after that. For a few months. I pushed myself not to absolve him of the responsibility that he so often avoided. I didn't want to call and make it all better. I didn't want us to merely move on as if nothing had transpired.

A month after our blowup, my father fell ill and ended up in the hospital. We talked then, but I was still conflicted. About a month after that, things became steadier. A few months after that, I went home for a visit.

I can't say that there was ever this grand conversation of closure. Of him owning anything. But there was truth. And time to sit with it. With no retraction of the way that I felt. And that was a lot. It was something that I needed. The lifting of that weight was for me – even if it was for me alone.

I know that my father loves me. I know that he always has. I understand that he has always done what he felt was his best. And his best was light-years ahead of what his father had given him. This I know. I know that his love for me was gentler and closer than the form of love his mother was able to give him. I know that the care he took in giving me exposure to so many things that would shape and open my mind was his expression of love.

I know that the time he spent with me, the miles he drove to be with me on countless weekends before he even moved to South Carolina... the times that he would turn around and come back when he couldn't fathom the thought of me crying nonstop after he left… that was love. I understand that my father has given me the best that he's known how.

My father would tell me that it was me who actually taught him how to love. He said that as a baby, I would hold his face in the palms of my little hands and say, "I love you, Daddy." He said that I would say it over and over until he said it back to me. I was relentless. To this day, I love my daddy. And the older I get, the more I experience, the more I seek an understanding of my past and my lineage – the better I understand the human condition. We all do the best we can.

11

THE STORY OF MY MOTHER

"Your hand is my hand. Your heart is my heart. Your eyes see what I see." Jaz Karis, "Sunrise"

Another beautiful result of my healing was eventually having the fortitude to survey who my mother was – no matter how emotionally taxing that exploration might prove to be. I eventually found the courage to dig deeper into understanding my mother's life – her spirit. This choice didn't come immediately. It was 2019 when I finally decided to begin that journey.

It had always been, at most, bearable for me to hear stories of her told when I was in earshot. To laugh at beautiful memories or hurt for her when I heard of things that were painful. As strong as I am, it's always been more tolerable for me to ignore things that leave me frail and exposed, such as my mother's story – that would be too heavy for me.

A year before my move to the Bay Area, my uncle sent me boxes and boxes of my mother's things. My grandfather had passed away in February 2015, and Poppy was moving to a different home.

To help with the move, my Uncle Reggie was cleaning out the shed that was in my grandparents' backyard and found many of my mother's things. It was as if her adult life had been suspended in place. There were so many things: wallets, letters, pictures, purses, college materials, to-do lists. There was so much that had always been there – saved for decades.

Reggie called me in tears, letting me know how much of my mother had been left behind in those boxes. He told me that I needed to see them. That it would be helpful for me to see who my mother was. I told him that I would like to have the items. That he should send them to me.

When I received those boxes, it was much harder to go through them than I anticipated. I wanted to receive them, yet I couldn't bring myself to open anything. It was too scary for me to open myself up to what I might feel, despite the beauty I might uncover amongst her things.

That was late 2015. In June of 2016, when my life exploded, I shipped the boxes of my mother's things with me to the Bay Area, as well as an armoire of my mother's that my dad had saved for me all my life.

When I set up my new life, I placed the armoire in my bedroom and stored my mother's items inside the drawers. There was so much. Just my fingertips touching the same things that she had once held felt so beautiful and so sad at the same time.

As I transferred things, I came across a wallet of

hers. I opened the wallet and tucked in front was a picture of Corey and my mother in a warm embrace. She loved Corey.

There was a time, years ago, when I asked Corey if he remembered our mother. We were both in high school – so it must have been circa 2004, when I was fourteen and Corey was seventeen.

"Of course I do, Casey," Corey said. "I remember her voice, her smell – "

I told him I couldn't take it. That hurt. My heart hurt for her. A twenty-one-year-old woman who had so much more life to live. Attached to children and family and loved ones. A woman with a voice, a smell, a whole life in front of her. My heart hurt for us. It hurt for Corey.

Corey, like my father, is an introvert. He's not one to express emotion often. For him to remember so many intricate details of my mother – for that to come from him… it broke my heart. I couldn't imagine what that loss must have felt like for him.

I told my dad that story – that Corey said that he

remembers our mother. That he remembered everything... down to her smell. I told him how painful that was to hear. My dad then told me a story.

He said that after my mother's death, Corey didn't seem to have much of a reaction. But, a year or two later, Corey and I went back to my dad's apartment. The same apartment that we all lived in as a family before my mother's death.

My dad said that when we got out of the car, Corey ran to the apartment door. He remembered that apartment. He remembered where we once lived together.

My dad said that when he opened the door to the apartment, Corey ran in singing, "Mommy! Mommy! Mommy!"

He ran around the apartment searching for her. He bent down, looking under spaces, while laughing. He thought that she must have been hiding from him.

That hurt my dad so much. I was bawling just hearing of it.

My dad said that he told Corey that Mommy

wasn't there. That she wasn't coming back. He said that Corey just stopped talking. That he never responded. My dad didn't know what Corey felt. But Corey just stopped talking and searching.

That's heavy.

As I transferred my mother's things into her armoire that was now passed down to me, I still couldn't bear to go through her things. This was in 2016 – when I was trying with all my might to swallow every single thing that had happened to me and to regain a sense of normalcy.

Years later, however, I would sit with tears and take the time to look through the things that my mother had left behind. In 2019, I carefully began to go through as much as I could handle at a given sitting, but eventually I made my way through everything. The things I saw helped to flesh out who she was as a person. Years later, there was still so much life amongst her things.

I was immediately blown away by the many similarities that we shared. It was incredible to see that I could have so many commonalities with a person I had not had contact with for more than twenty-seven years. Like an old church song says, the blood never loses its power.

Looking at my mom's high school transcript was like looking at my own! AP English – 100, AP Calculus – 100, Physics – 100, AP Chemistry – 100, Government & Econ – 97, Adv. Oral Communication – 97, Office Assistant – 99. I had similar grades and a 5.094 GPA when I graduated. I'm so sure she would have been proud.

My mother graduated from Central High School in 1988. Everyone has told me that she was smart and spunky. According to my mom's yearbook comments, she was "like one of the boys," "half-crazy and half-intelligent," and would be remembered for "all of her boyfriends." Ha!

During January of her senior year, my mom was featured in the school newspaper as the Student of the Month. In the article, my mom shared that her favorite food was cheesecake and that her favorite singers were Billie Holiday, Jennifer Holliday, and Luther Vandross. Her fantasy was to cut a love song record with ex-Shalamar singer Howard Hewett, and her life goal was to live in a $60,000 house with a Jaguar, a Mercedes, and a Lamborghini all parked in the driveway.

My mom was the vice president of the National Honors Society, secretary of the Math Club, and the senior class executive of the Student Council. She was also a member of the Spanish Club, Central High School Chorus, and S.A.D.D.

In the same article, she was asked if she had any nicknames, to which she replied, "None that are publishable."

When asked to leave a final quote, she stated, "It is funny how people claim to feel one way about you, but then their actions say just the opposite (for example R.S.)."

I remember my Uncle Reggie telling me about a boyfriend of hers named R.S. Apparently, my mom had embarrassed this guy a few times that year for crossing her – he was an ex-boyfriend. I find it hilarious that my mom used her prime real estate in the school newspaper to further humiliate the young man. Pet-ty! Ha!

My mom was featured on another page of that same month's newspaper for being the district winner of the Voice of Democracy Contest in December 1987, a contest that involved writing an essay on American liberty and submitting a cassette tape recording. The article mentioned that she had also gone on to place third in the state competition thereafter. Her picture was shown, yet again, in that same newspaper for being nominated for an English award sponsored by the *Columbus Ledger Enquirer*. Mom was dope!

I had the pleasure of speaking with two of my mother's friends from college to learn more about her. Thanks to my dad, we were able to connect over Facebook. My dad had told me about them some year's prior, after discovering them on the networking site.

One of them, Penny, had asked my dad if it would be okay to reach out to me. Before I started going through my mother's things in 2019, I wasn't ready. The other, Shadé, was my mom's best friend. My dad had given me Shadé's name – but I just couldn't bring myself to reach out.

One weekend in the summer of 2019, however, as I sat in the middle of my bedroom floor, crying, surrounded by many of my mother's things – I wanted to connect. I wanted to know so much more.

I reached out to each of them, and they were thrilled to connect. Finally speaking to them helped to bring even more life and volume to the many items that my mom left behind. They were able to recount memories of her that made me laugh and beam with pride.

I learned that my mom had so much personality – it's insane how much I am like her. I would relay the stories her friends would share with me to my dad, sparking so much happiness and excitement in him. It made him reminisce on moments that he had long forgotten. Fun memories of college times. Memories of struggle and being broke and them not even realizing it. Delving into these stories was a beautiful and emotional experience for both of us.

My mom showed up at Georgia Tech in the fall of

1988 as a mechanical engineering major. That's where she met Penny, her college roommate. Penny and my mom didn't start off as roommates, but shortly after arriving on campus with neither of them getting along with their assigned roommates, they conspired to change rooms and share one together instead. They landed a room at the end of the hall, close to the stairwell – which felt like hitting the jackpot.

Penny said that she and my mom had such a great time together – they were both strong-willed, both engineering majors (one chemical, the other mechanical), and both loved partying! They would even plan their weekend outfits together during the school week!

Penny said that my mom loved colors. She'd wear nail polish and bangle bracelets. She had a signature black bubble skirt that she had gotten from her Aunt Edna, which would just kill folks at the parties.

Penny recounted that my grandparents were Seventh-day Adventists. She said that she could always tell when my grandparents were coming to visit, because my mom would remove her nail polish and hide all her fashionable hoopla. Oh, and she'd be wearing a skirt... but not the kill-em-at-the-parties-black-bubble-skirt. We're talking Seventh-day Adventist church skirt. Hilarious.

Penny and my mom really enjoyed their freshman year at Georgia Tech. From stories of peach schnapps and Everclear, to habitually getting parking tickets and having their cars impounded, there was rarely a dull moment with my mom, she said.

Penny mentioned that there was another side to my mom as well. Aside from the fun-spirited nature, aside from the ambitious grit – my mom had a deep, aged soul. My dad would tell me the same thing. That she seemed a lot older than she really was. That she had a seriousness about her at times... and seemed to carry some sadness that she didn't want to share. A sadness that stemmed from her childhood.

At times, Penny would walk into the dorm room and find my mom in the dark singing somber songs by artists like Nina Simone or Billie Holiday. One day, Penny walked in on my mom singing "Strange Fruit," and she finally had to call her out.

"Wanda, are you okay?" she asked.

My mom chuckled and said, "Oh girl, don't pay me any mind. I do this sometimes. Don't mind me."

My mom's best friend in college was named Shadé, who was also an engineering major. Shadé described my mother as being extremely frank, a straight shooter, and a true friend. She said that my mom was perceptive and could really read people. She could size a person up and determine a sense of their character pretty quickly.

When Shadé and my mom began hanging out, my mom looked her over and said to her one day, "My mom wouldn't like you."

Shadé grew up practicing her Muslim faith. On top of that, she was from Florida. According to my mom, between that religion and being from such a racy place – that was sure to put my mom's new best friend on the "no" list. Shadé thought this especially funny since this Seventh-day Adventist "church girl" was schooling her on the ropes while starting college!

Shadé said that my mother taught her street smarts. She took her first drink with my mom.

"Don't just drink with anybody, Shadé," my mom told her. "You need to only drink around people that you know. People that you trust!"

Hearing these stories was so funny! They reminded me so much of my freshman year experiences at the University of South Carolina. While I didn't start off the school year with a roommate, my now good friend Toya and I submitted a request to room together.

I had started in a tiny dorm room by myself, just as I had requested but then found that I hated the solitude. I can't remember what happened to Toya's initial roommate —nonetheless, our mutual friend Jackie introduced us to one another, recommending that we try rooming together to solve both our dorm problems.

Similar to the stories from Penny and Shadé about my mom, I was this church girl schooling Toya. Both Toya and I were in the Honors College, both strong-willed, and both of us had big plans for our futures.

I remember going out to the club with Toya one night.

"Toya, if you drink anything tonight – don't let the bouncers see you," I said.

We were having a good time, dancing and vibing, when in what felt like slow motion, I see Toya standing in the middle of the dance floor with a jumbo syringe filled with a Jell-O shot, and she's rearing her head back to plunge in her mouth. On her wrist was a bright green band, signifying that she was underage.

I ran over to block Toya, but before I could get to her, a security officer had grabbed her by the arm and threw both of us out into the back alley! Ha! Good times.

Anyway, Shadé and my mom were thick as thieves. She said that my mom was not a wallflower when they would go out – she would not blend in with the crowd. My mom was full of life and could light up any room.

Similar to what Penny had described, though, she

mentioned that it seemed my mom was going through things that she would never talk about. She would have these odd moments of sadness at times, but then snap out of it and shrug it off – quickly pivoting back to her jovial demeanor.

Shadé even recounted a time when they found my mom passed out on the dorm floor. Her skin red, she had a tan line on her legs from where her legs had been exposed to the sun. Penny brought up this day with me as well – the day that my mom seemed odd.

When my mom came to, she said she had been at Piedmont Park all day, then shrugged it off. She managed to lighten the mood, forcefully changing the subject – but everyone felt a little strange about that day. They apparently still do all these years later.

My dad says it was the first day of the spring semester when my mom first noticed him. My dad was a brother of Kappa Alpha Psi, and he and his fraternity were performing at the Greek Step Show that was held in March of 1989. Shadé happened to be a Kappa Sweetheart.

"Who is that brother with the big butt?" my mom

asked Shadé.

After the show, Shadé told my dad that she had a friend who was interested in him. A large group of them went out to a late night Tex-Mex spot that night, and that was my dad's first time meeting my mom. They exchanged information and planned to meet up a few days later.

On the day that my dad and mom were supposed to meet, my mom didn't call, and my dad was unable to get in touch with her. After learning from Shadé that she was at her dorm room, he walked in as they were all looking at my mom on the floor, after she had just regained consciousness.

My dad said that even after something so frightening, my mom managed to gain control of the room, telling everyone to chill. She was cracking jokes, distracting everyone from her incident. My dad said he said to himself, *Man, this girl is interesting.* Lol! It was from that point forward they began dating. This also happened to be his first time meeting my grandparents. They showed up to her dorm room from Alabama after learning about what had happened.

My dad already had a son at this point, who was about a year and a half – my brother, Corey. Things moved quickly with my mom and dad, more quickly than either of them likely would have imagined when they first met.

Among my mother's things, I found a Residence Hall Space Contract for Fulmer Hall for the upcoming fall. She had signed the contract in April of 1989. Georgia Tech was on a quarter system then, so my mother returned to her parents' house in Alabama that June when the quarter ended, expecting to return to Atlanta in September. While my mom would return to Atlanta, it wouldn't be under the same circumstances she had originally planned.

Amongst her things, I found a handwritten letter my mother had written to my father, but never sent. It was dated June 11, 1989. In this letter, she suspects that she is pregnant. While her first pregnancy test had come back negative, she wasn't sure if she trusted the results, as her breasts had almost doubled in size and her appetite was a lot larger. She suspected it might have been too early to get a positive read, so she would wait a week to retake the test, and if it came back positive, she figured she'd be a month into her term. The end of the letter read as such:

> *At times, I think of us – you, me Corey and "?" as a family. And I think of how happy we would be together. I miss you so much. I think of you constantly. I want to kiss you and touch you so much, but I try not to think about it because I can't. I'm starting to miss you even more just writing about it. I don't want to get depressed, so I'll close now and drown my sorrows in food. Just kidding! But I could use a snack. Take care of yourself and think of me – think of us. Remember I love you very, very much and if you give me a chance, I'll take good care of you and little DK. I'll talk to you again soon.*
>
> *Love always,*
>
> *Wanda*

"DK" is the pronunciation of my maiden name "Diké" I used to write my last name as DK when social media first became a thing – so that people knew the correct pronunciation.

A few weeks later, my mom received a letter from Shadé dated June 30, 1989. It's funny to think about how people were restricted to communicating via letters and collect calls back then. The Internet wouldn't be created until 1991, and calls across state lines were not free of charge in those days.

In the letter, Shadé is letting my mom know that she had received my mom's initial letter to her and that she was so happy to hear from her. Shadé dishes the latest about her boy drama and wishes my mom luck on her "weekend with Chinaka's family." Chinaka is my dad, though he most often goes by his middle name – Albert.

She tells my mom to tell my dad hi for her and tells her that she "really hopes to see her in Atlanta in the fall." The letter wraps up:

Take care of yourself and girlfriend keep in touch. I'm going to do my part about keeping in touch, so the pressure is on you. Make an effort, because I will ('cause I really value our friendship).

Love ya,

Shadé

My mother and father were married that next month on July 28, 1989. My dad, mom, and Corey moved into a one-bedroom apartment in Atlanta, Georgia. My mom loved Corey so very much. Poppy would tell me stories of my mom having Corey all dressed up for church and how he would come in, his arm dangling from hers, his legs just-a-moving!

My grandmother would ask my mom, "What's going to happen to Corey if you and Albert don't make it?"

My grandmother said that my mom would look her square in the eyes and say, "He's mine – I'll raise him!"

I told my dad that story, and he chuckled. "And she meant that!" he said.

From what I can tell from looking through my mother's things, she had made a resolute decision that she would not be returning to Georgia Tech that fall.

I found a note that my mother had jotted down on two small rectangular pieces of paper. It read:

Dear Sir

I am one of the Kodak Scholars enrolled at the Georgia Institute of Technology as a freshman. During my first year of college, I became more knowledgeable of the roles of mechanical engineering and have decided that I no longer wish to pursue a career in mechanical engineering. I desire to cancel my scholarship.

Your assistance is gre

That's where the note ends. She didn't write anything else after "gre."

If I am anything like my mother, I can only suspect that she took some drastic measure to course-correct her life in the way that she deemed necessary and important to her. She chose her path. Yes, she was young – nineteen years old. But she made a choice for her life, and she carried it all the way through.

I was born February 13, 1990. When I was really

young, I remember being told that my mother intentionally scheduled her C-section to occur on the 13th of the month because Corey's birthday is August 13th. She wanted us to always know that we were brother and sister.

My mom detailed the first year of my life in a book that I found among her things. I told my dad how she'd logged so many of my moments in that first year, creating lines and adding to the preset list of only nine "Important Dates" given in my children's book.

"She did it for you," my dad said in an assured and soothing tone. His response sent shivers through my soul.

As written about me in my mother's log:

- 02-13-90: First smile

- 02-20-90: Turns head while lying on stomach

- 02-22-90: First laugh

- 03-31-90: Sleeps all night

- 06-04-90: Spits

- 06-19-90: Puts hands together in play

- 07-07-90: First plays with feet while lying on back

- 07-07-90: First puts pacifier in mouth by herself

- 08-06-90: First Word ("Da Da")

- 08-08-90: First holds bottle by herself

- 08-24-90: Sits alone

- 09-19-90: Rolls over

- 10-03-90: First tooth (First tooth broke through her gums. Lower right middle tooth. Could see lower left middle tooth underneath the gum. Nothing at the top.)

- 10-30-90: Pulls self up

- 11-01-90: Crawls (First time without stomach on the ground)

- 12-02-90: First stands without holding onto anything

- 12-25-90: She surprises everyone by drinking from a straw

- 12-26-90: Stands about eleven seconds on her own. She sat down when she realized everyone was watching.

- 12-26-90: Over the Thanksgiving break, Christina taught Casey how to say "what," but Casey couldn't pronounce it clearly enough to convince anyone else she could say it. But on this day, she even accented the "t" sound when she said it and my dad almost couldn't believe it. Everyone thought it sounded so cute.

- 03-27-91: Walks (Christy and Reggie were visiting for Spring Break)

I turned one on February 13, 1991. My mom wanted to make sure that day was absolutely special for me – even if it was just her, Corey, and myself at the apartment. I was turning one! My dad was at work that day, but my mom filled the kitchen with balloons and birthday cards, making sure the house looked festive enough for me to realize there was something special taking place that day.

My mom pulled out giant chocolate chip ice cream sandwiches and placed them in front of Corey and me. She took photos of us marveling at the mountain of sweetness placed in front of us and then diving in with our fingers to work at eating the cold, sweet treat.

That day was special to my mother. Every day with me was special. She hung on to my every action. She found joy in everything I did. My grandmother would tell me that my mom loved spending time with me and would get so tickled by my sense of awareness at such a young age.

My grandmother said my mom would often laugh and say to her, "I think this girl *knows* what she's doing!"

Penny told me a similar story, saying my mom was convinced that I knew how to walk earlier than I would let on. She would laugh and say I was walking behind her back – because there was just no way I was moving as fast as I was across the room without walking.

Wanda,

Hey gurl! How are you? Fine I hope. I just got your letter today and I was so happy to hear from you.

Well enough about this place. I really hope things are working out for you. I really hope to see you in Atlanta in the fall. I hope your weekend with Chiraka's family turns out ok. Say hi to him for me. Take care of yourself and girlfriend keep in touch. I'm going to be my part about keeping in touch so the pressure on you. Make an effort because I will (cause I really value our friendship).

Love Ya
Shatè

June 11, 1999
Sunday

Chinaka,

This is kind of strange for me to write you. I guess its because I've never talked to you on paper, and you're never seen my sloppy handwriting. well, it is late at night and I am in pain, so it decided to write you to get off the pain. I love all of you because I used to help it out infirmary. When the pain assumed C and the pain, I from just thinking of you so much. So not as lonely when be calling a new and I need you so much and physically replacing you a...

I feel all the time, and how my throat and change my symptoms and I feel lumps in my breasts forming that seems never they I either the but that isn't incared, this being is going to be surge it. something is surely only with me. From talk to live long.... on I guess about being back over hate for a sometimes I feel like living myself into life I just be my for is to handle. But I know it will get hard, tight and make it through. being, Amy and it will be alright. We will do it together. At times I think it is - something - and I think of how happy we could be together. I miss you constantly. I went to kiss you, and touch you so much but I try not to think about it very even worse. I'm starting to miss you even more just writing about it. I don't want to get replaced at all that and know... and know. I'm going back in good. I Just missing you. But I would tell it so much. Take care of yourself and think of me. I'll take care of me... I love you very very much love love of you and ache and little life will talk to you soon.

Love Always,
Lianda

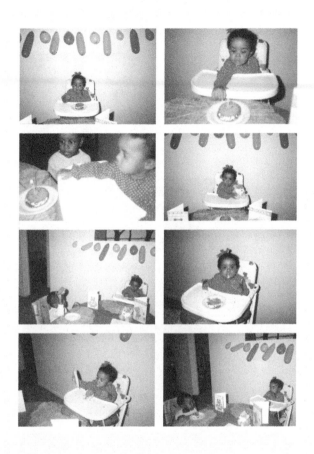

Though my mom found happiness in loving Corey, my father, and me, there were still times that she withdrew, seeking solitude. Even while she was pregnant with me, my mom would sometimes retreat into a dark room by herself. My dad mentioned this to me a few times as I was growing up.

He said that she would sing to me. That she would often go off and talk to me alone when I was still in her belly. He believed that she would say things to me in those moments that she wouldn't even share with him. She had a weight from her childhood and her adulthood that she carried with her. Heartache that she wouldn't share with her circle in Atlanta.

After my mom had died, my dad remembers a time that I started singing a song that my mother used to sing to me. I didn't even know that I was doing it – but it startled him because he had not heard that song since my mother was alive... which had been over a year at this point.

"What were you singing?" he asked me.

He said that I looked confused, that I didn't even realize I had been singing. He said he never heard me sing that song again. He thought it was powerful that song was still somehow a part of me. I find it powerful that so much of my mother is still a part of me. Her pain and her wit. Her will and her stubbornness. Her magnetic persona and her loneliness. It's absolutely incredible.

By all accounts, my mother was a beautiful person. She loved me… dearly. She loved both Corey and me. She meant so much to so many people.

She was abruptly taken away in June of 1991, four months after my first birthday. That morning, my mom left the apartment to sell Avon products while my dad stayed at home to watch Corey and me. The plan was for my mom to come home early enough to relieve my dad for work that afternoon.

My mom didn't make it home in time for my father to go to work. Because of this, my dad knew that something was wrong. He knew that she wouldn't leave her children unattended. He knew it.

My mom was missing without a single trace. Despite my father's attempts to get authorities involved, the police refused to send out a search party for her since she hadn't been missing for a full twenty-four hours.

My dad didn't need twenty-four hours to go by to know that something had gone terribly wrong. She wouldn't have abandoned Corey and me. He just knew that she wouldn't.

With hardly any options, my father went walking around the apartment complex to search for her. He tried to retrace the steps she might have taken on her route to sell the Avon products. As he was walking outside, he smelled my mother's fragrance trailing in the wind.

My dad followed his nose and it led him to the dumpster of our apartment complex. His heart stopped. He knew that it was her smell. Just as he knew that something had gone terribly wrong. He stood paralyzed. Not understanding whether this was reality or some horrible nightmare.

My father stepped forward and opened the lid of

the dumpster, the smell growing even more potent. My father searched inside and found a bag with my mother's clothes inside.

With the bag now in possession, the police jumped to search for her. With the police now on the case, my father called home to my family in Alabama.

My Uncle Reggie remembers answering the phone when my dad called to say that my mom was missing. Reggie said that when he picked up the phone and heard the pause from the other end, he knew something terrible had happened to my mom. My family rushed to Atlanta as they searched for the body.

The bag that my father found eventually led the police to my mother's body and her killer. The murderer was sick. He had chopped parts of my mother's body, stuffed her inside a box, and hid that box inside his closet.

The details of my mother's murder were horrific. She had shown up to an apartment to sell Avon products to an older woman who would often buy items from her. Unbeknownst to my mother, this woman's son had recently been released from prison, after being charged with the brutal rape and assault of a woman. The man had left this woman so battered and mentally frail that she could barely testify in court. He was deranged and ordered to take medication for his mental state while living with his mother.

Unfortunately for my mother, it was this man who opened the door – not his mother. The investigation indicated that there was a struggle sometime inside that apartment. My mother tried her best to fight him off. I've heard an account or two of her having gotten the best of him and rushing to the door to get out of the apartment – at which time he grabbed her from behind and then suffocated her to death.

Though my mother fought back, she never made it out of that apartment. It was this scene that replayed over and over in my head the night my ex-husband abused me. I kept thinking about how she tried her best to fight back, but still never made it out alive.

For this reason, I would not hit my husband back that night he abused me. The rage that I saw in his eyes was foreign, yet eerily familiar. I just knew... I just *knew* he was capable of killing me if I were to incite any more rage from him. My goal was making it out of that house alive. And to never, ever, look back.

My mom's death left my entire family reeling. All of us. None of our lives were ever the same. I am still working to cope with the aftermath of her death as an adult today.

12

ONE DAY YOU'LL FLY

"My day is coming… it won't be like this always. I'm one more tear closer – it washes away the pain." – Casey Ariel (circa 2002), "My Day is Coming"

I was always a strong and capable student. I worked hard, made straight As, and stayed out of trouble, which often gained me the favor and attention of teachers and faculty at my schools. When

I was in fifth grade, without knowing it or being acutely aware, a teacher of mine gifted me with a compass that would guide me throughout the rest of my life.

"Casey, I want you to learn 'The Creed' by Marva Collins it in its entirety."

She handed me these sheets of paper filled with words. There were so many words. I flipped through the papers and looked back up at her.

"Okay, Ms. Haney."

She smiled at me, light dancing in her eyes as it always did.

"I see your name in lights, Casey," she would tell me. "I see your name in lights."

Ms. Haney always saw so much in me. I instinctively knew that she saw me as being as limitless as I felt. There has always been this burning strength and purpose inside me that I felt was meant to touch the world – a feeling that I recognized even at a young age.

I learned that piece. I spent the entirety of my

weeklong spring break in Alabama practicing it over
and over and over. Until it stuck.

Society will draw a circle that shuts me out
But my superior thoughts will draw me in

I was born to win
If I do not spend too much time trying to fail

I can become a citizen of this world
If I do not spend too many energies attempting to
become a local

I will ignore the tags and names given me by society
Since only I know what I have the ability to become

I will continue to let society predict
But only I can determine what I will, can and cannot
do

Failure is just as easy to combat as success is to obtain

Education is painful and not gained by playing games
But I, too, have seen failure destroy millions with

promised hopes and broken dreams

While I have the opportunity, I shall not sit on the sidelines broken with despair
And later wish that I had become a literate lifter of this world instead of a failing leaner

I will use each day to the fullest
I promise that each day will be gained, not lost
Used, not thrown away

Yet it is my privilege to destroy myself if that is what I choose to do

I have the right to fail, but I do not have the right to bring my teachers and others down with me

I am the captain of my own life
Therefore, if I decide to become a failure, that is my right

We are all promised the pursuit of happiness, and that is what I must do

Pursue happiness and success for myself

No one will give it to me on a proverbial platter
And no one will care as much about me as much as I
must care about myself

But I must be willing to accept the consequences for
that failure
And must never think that those who have chosen to
work
While I have slept rested and played
Will share their bounties with me

I will wave proudly my flag, signifying that I am a
failure by choice
But will never envy those who have chosen their
unfurled banners announcing their success

My success and my education can be a companion
Which no misfortune can depress
No crime can destroy
No enemy can alienate
No envy or names can hurt me

Education and success can be a lifetime solace

It guides goodness

It gives grace and genius to governments, communities,

cities, townships, villages homes and palaces

Without education, what is a man

A splendid slave

A savage

A beast

Wandering from here to there, believing whatever they

are told

God is not some cosmic bellboy who comes at my every

beckon and call

If I want to achieve the first step must be my own

undertaking

Likewise, if I want to fail that, too, is my choice

Time and chance come to us all

Whether I decide to take that time and chance is

indeed my choice

I can either be hesitant or courageous
Life does indeed maroon the hesitant and inspire the
brave

I can swiftly stand up and shout, "This is my time
and my place.

I will accept the challenge

Or I will let others
make my decisions
for me."

I recited "The Creed" at my fifth grade graduation with more conviction than anyone would have imagined could come from an eleven-year old girl. Those words meant everything to me. They were a guide. They held life keys for me, and I knew it.

I wanted to escape a reality that was unfortunate and painful. And with these words now internalized, I knew I wouldn't let anything about my circumstance break my spirit. That one day, I would fly above all of the horrible experiences that had happened in my life. I learned to step over pain early in my life and, from then on, the words from "The Creed" became a playbook for me.

I recited "The Creed" the very next year as a sixth grader in my middle school pageant, winning the entire pageant. I was named "Miss Southeast Middle School" and "Miss Congeniality" that year.

"The Creed" stuck with me. It taught me how to behave, how to push past, how to identify decisions as my own – those decisions resistant to committee or buy-in. Almost two decades later, I can still recite those words by memory.

I knew how to press on. I had grit. I had tenacity. All of which served me well. I was named valedictorian of my fifth grade, eighth grade, and twelfth grade classes. Stepping from one milestone to the next on my way out.

When I was graduating from high school, one of

my elementary school teachers paid me a visit. Ms. Rockledge was her name. She had been my pre-K teacher and taught me again in the fourth and fifth grades for Advanced Academic Program (AAP) math and English classes.

Ms. Rockledge had long since moved away from South Carolina. Her husband had shot her in an attempt to kill her right before turning the gun on himself, committing suicide. She was paralyzed from the waist down as a result of that incident and had moved far away to Pennsylvania.

Though I had not seen or spoken to her in years, Ms. Rockledge came all the way back to South Carolina to see me graduate from high school. After the graduation, she asked me if we could go out to lunch the next day. I agreed, of course, feeling very humbled and appreciative that she would come such a long way to see me walk across the graduation stage and speak to me before I went off to college.

As I sat across the lunch table from Ms. Rockledge, tears filled her eyes.

"I am so proud of you, Casey. You are so strong.

You are such a strong girl."

I was confused. I mean, I *was* strong. But I didn't have any reason to believe that she would have taken note of that. Not in any way that would have caused her to cry as she looked at me all those years later.

"Ms. Rockledge, what's wrong? Why are you crying?"

Ms. Rockledge's tears kept coming. She began shaking her head, still looking me in my eyes. Something pained her. Something that she really wanted to say. I am not sure if she was trying to find the words or battling whether to say what she had intended after coming such a long way.

"You made it through that horrible situation, Casey."

I frowned. *What could she have been talking about? I'd never complained at school. I'd kept it cool. What was she talking about?*

Ms. Rockledge took a deep breath.

"Before children start our pre-kindergarten program, we go by their homes for a visit. We like to take a look at the living conditions and assess their environment. Oh, Casey…"

She began sobbing. Putting her hands over her mouth.

I was frozen. I was completely frozen. I didn't understand what I was feeling in that moment. I didn't know what to name it. To be honest, I was wishing that I didn't feel anything at all.

I sat there, gazing back without much reaction. Not knowing what to do with the feelings that I had. Not knowing whether to show any response. Whether to show curiosity. Whether to show my own internalized sadness. The sadness that had been there all along.

"It's okay, Ms. Rockledge."

"No. Casey, you didn't even have a bed. She didn't even have a bed for you to sleep in."

Tears came running down my face, though I kept the same blank expression. I had not remembered this. But it was sad. It was heartbreaking.

I was sitting across the table from a woman who

was crying for that little girl. A woman who was crying for *me*. She saw me. She saw the tragic state that I was in, while it seemed to be invisible to so many around me.

Why wasn't I protected? Why didn't anyone care about this? Why wasn't I saved? Whose job was it to step in to help this little girl?

Ms. Rockledge wept as if there was an apology in her eyes. I sat, staring back at her, tears running down my face – but not making a movement. Not giving her a reply.

She went on.

"Casey, you were always so smart. You were so smart. So much so, that there were times that I believed you would intentionally try to correct me in front of the class. I wanted to correct that behavior. I wanted to steer you from behaving in such a way, so I told her. I had to. I didn't know that she would do that to you."

I continued to stare back at her. Tears were flowing, but I composed myself. I didn't want her to see me visibly impacted. I didn't want to show her brokenness. I was going to rise above all of this. *Who was going to protect this girl when no one else would? I would. I would protect this little girl. I was almost there.*

She talked about the way that Aunt Rose slapped my face in front of her the day that she was called into the conference to discuss the incident. She talked about how horrified she was. She mentioned how much she regretted placing me in that situation. She expressed her sorrow for seeing me in such a situation.

"It's okay, Ms. Rockledge. She didn't break me. I'm going to make it. One day, I'll be free from all of this. She won't be able to hurt me."

I wiped my tears, and we finished our lunch.

13

FAIRY TALES & NIGHTMARES

"We built sandcastles... that washed away." – Beyoncé,
"Sandcastles"

I remember the day that Aaron and I got married like it was yesterday. It was June 2, 2012, just four weeks after I had graduated from the University of South Carolina. I was stepping into so many things at once. Adulthood. Womanhood. Leaving my hometown for the first time on a permanent basis. Corporate America. Marriage.

So many things were happening, but I was completely unafraid. My soon-to-be-husband was my high school sweetheart. We had practically grown up together. I loved that man. There was so much about him to love. The compassion that he had in his heart for people. His athleticism and connection to the community. His humility and gratitude for the simple things.

I loved that he adored and respected me. I appreciated that, for the six years that we dated, he valued my choice for abstinence. I loved the way that he loved me.

Aaron's love and prioritization for family was primary in his life. Aaron was one of nine children: the middle child. He and his siblings had been through a lot and were extremely protective of one another. I admired their closeness. Watching him with his nieces and nephews, I believed that he would be an incredible father in the future. Equipped to give love and protection.

I saw my own grandfather in Aaron's eyes. He, like my grandfather, aspired to be the first person in his immediate family to obtain a college degree. He held a deep desire to lift and help the people he loved. He was a beautiful spirit, even though there were things that I didn't fully understand about him at the time. Serious issues that I had no idea he was battling… even after all those years of dating.

I remember us both sobbing at the Columbia airport when he was flying off to basic training for the Airforce National Guard. He was joining so that he could get help paying for school. Family members that he loved and looked up to had done the same before him, but, boy, was he nervous! We hugged and cried and waved each other goodbye until we were out of each other's sight.

About a year later, Aaron would come to Charlotte to visit me during my finance internship in the summer before my senior year of college. We were engaged to be married by that point. Aaron had proposed sometime after returning from basic training.

That summer, Aaron and I smiled so big the first time we were able to sit down at a restaurant and order an appetizer and a full meal. That was living.

At the end of my internship, I received a job offer to return to Charlotte full-time post-graduation, so that was our plan. To marry and head to Charlotte.

During the years we dated, we would often hold hands and dream about the life we would have together. We would speak aloud about how we envisioned ourselves sitting in the living room of our own house one day, holding one another.

We would talk about how we would have a little girl and name her Erin Faith, so that she could have his namesake. Faith would be her middle name because it was the substance of things hoped for and the evidence of things not seen. Erin Faith would be our first child, we decided. Her brothers would be named Preston Kyle and Justin Michael. Preston would be the smart, obedient one. And Justin, that Justin would be a handful. But we would love all three of them and pour ourselves into each.

We talked about how we would give our children a

life that would be absent of the gaps that we both felt in our own upbringing. We would take everything that we were – a product of the villages that raised us – and pour that and even more into a family of our own.

We loved one another. We had it all planned out. The first step was to get married at a church in a small South Carolina town, barely a mile away from where I had grown up.

I surprised Aaron by singing to him on our wedding day. I was shy about singing solos back then. I sang in a traveling band, I would sing at church, I would sing duets at weddings every now and then… but I was very shy about performing alone.

But for him… I would. When it was time for me to walk down the aisle on my wedding day, I appeared at the entryway of the sanctuary, singing the words from the song "Golden" by Chrisette Michele:

I'm so ready to love / I'm so ready to promise my all

I'm so ready to give 'til the day that my life is no more

We got married and had a huge reception in "the city," which is what we called Columbia. After the reception, we were picked up by a horse-drawn carriage and taken to The Inn – a beautiful boutique hotel on the University of South Carolina's campus. I became a woman on this day, fully giving myself to the love of my life. It was a fairytale come true.

I thought for sure that our lives would be blissful as we walked off into the sunset. Surely we'd stay together forever, have our three children, whom we would love very much, and be an example for all to follow.

Despite all that had transpired in my life up to that point, I would now have control over the entirety of my life. I had committed to everything that mattered to me in my life: my faith, my education, my partner, my future. I had remained focused and diligent. Now I was leaving South Carolina to start my life – finally independent.

After our honeymoon in Montego Bay, Jamaica, we would touch back down in Charlotte, North

Carolina. We had already set up our first apartment in South Park – the historical and financially wealthy area of Charlotte. South Park had beautiful lawns, clean streets, families pushing strollers, people out on jogs in the morning. After six years of dating, we had done it. Stepping into matrimony, we were finally building the life we had always dreamed of.

Some years later, I remember a time in which I was so tired, all I could do was lay sobbing on our dining room floor. It was one of the few moments that I allowed myself to say aloud that I felt sorry for myself. There was so much weight that I was under.

In May of 2015, my husband was laid off. The next twelve months proved to be turbulent. He would never manage to get back on his feet. He'd get a job and then be laid off again. He'd get another job offer, and then I'd check the mail and learn that his offer had been rescinded because he'd refused to complete the pre-employment activities that were required.

I'd open the correspondence to learn of this truth after weeks of him pretending to go into work. He had been getting fully dressed in the mornings and kissing me goodbye, as if he was actually going into work.

I found myself on the floor screaming and sobbing after finding out about a woman that he had been seeing a few months prior. I wanted to leave him then. I told him that I would. I bought a plane ticket to Miami to be with both of my best friends, Hope and Monnie, for a few days, and I pulled myself together enough to get my exit plan together during the weekend of my twenty-sixth birthday.

I planned to leave Aaron then. After he walked into the house at 5:00 a.m. on the day before my birthday and admitted that he had been with her. A cold side of him had shown up then. He refused to leave. His rebuttal – "I'm not going anywhere, you leave!"

I didn't recognize this man. I flew to Miami the next morning, and my best friends met me there with open arms. I couldn't believe what was happening.

There were tears – there were so many tears. There was so much pain. But even then, I was moved to muster up the rationale to leave him. I deserved better. I was a good woman. I'd loved this man with my whole heart for almost a decade, only for him to betray me.

As soon as I landed in Miami and my phone regained cellular connection, my phone was buzzing with messages from a church member. At that time, I was heavily involved with my church. I sang each Sunday on the praise and worship team, often leading praise and worship songs. These commitments helped develop my close relationship with the church's minister of music.

She was calling and texting me, pleading to speak with me. Pleading for me to pray. Letting me know over and over again that I was in covenant and that this situation was not mine to end in isolation. That God had the final say. That she could attest that God could kill the spirit of adultery and lust. She beckoned me to seek spiritual counseling, rather than end my marriage.

My response to her was that infidelity was not love. That I understood that many women in the church were accustomed to and accepted that behavior from their husbands – but that was not something I was interested in doing. I responded that while I loved my husband, I loved myself – and no one was going to love me more than I loved myself. I would set the standard for what I would accept in my marriage.

While I was getting pleas on one side to not break our marriage covenant with God, my Aunt Christy was calling to tell me that I deserved better. To not listen to the women in church who wanted me to do what they had done. She told me that my choice was the right one. She told me that she would help me do whatever I needed to do to leave and start on my own.

My husband was reaching out too, apologizing – asking me to come home. Letting me know that God would work it out. That he was praying for me to forgive him. But on our Verizon account, I could see the outgoing calls and messages that he was making to the other woman. I could see that he was communicating with her even more than he was communicating with me.

I was so hurt. Inwardly, I knew that I deserved better. I knew that I deserved goodness. I knew that I was a loving wife. I knew that I had been supportive and sacrificed everything I had in efforts to bridge us over financially while he was supposed to be getting back on his feet.

Things were extremely off since that previous May. I didn't want to displease God. While I had never encountered anyone who left their husband the first time they cheated – I'd always said that I would. I knew I couldn't be any other woman. I didn't have any other version of myself to offer in order to keep him entertained. If I was no longer enough to satiate him – that was that. That said, I continued to battle with the idea of counseling before calling it quits.

After a few days, having retrieved the number of the woman from our Verizon call log, I texted her.

Are you sleeping with my husband?

The number called me immediately. I answered.

The woman was out of breath.

"Your what?!"

"My husband," I said.

"He can't be married! He can't be married! He is with me every day!"

I let her know that couldn't be the case because Aaron was with me every day. She was out of breath... she sounded very winded.

She let me know that Aaron would come over to her house every morning after he got off work. She said that he worked night shift.

I chuckled and said, "He doesn't have a job."

She couldn't believe it! She let me know that he must have been spending my money. She said that he would pick her four kids up from school every day. That he would buy Pampers and other things for them. That he was just at a birthday party the weekend prior and helped put all of the toys on the back of his Dodge Ram to take back to "the house."

The very same day my husband told me that he was away helping to run the sound at a church function, he was celebrating a child's birthday with his side family.

The woman was very apologetic. She mentioned that she would see a "Casey" call Aaron at times and that he would say he had an uncle named Casey. Aaron would never let her come to his house because *apparently* he lived in a bachelor pad and the fellas were junky. That so-called bachelor pad was our beautiful two-story home that we had built together from the ground up.

I let her know that I planned to leave him and that I would need whatever information she could offer in order to build my case to prove his infidelity. At this time, having not consulted a lawyer, I was unaware I would need to be legally separated from Aaron for a year before filing for the divorce, regardless of the circumstance.

This woman agreed to assist and sent me screenshots of their conversations, pictures, etc. I filed these away as evidence.

When I made it back from Miami, Aaron was at home. I tried to play it cool. I tried to remain calm, but hearing him plead and act as if he were really praying to the Lord to fix everything annoyed me beyond composure.

I yelled at him for all of the lies and sneaking and treating me the way that he had.

He was so angry he punched his fist through the bathroom door, inches from where I stood. He yelled, "I waited for you for six years, and you can't be patient with me for a few months?"

I was so shocked. Who was this person? How had this become my life? How was I the person that was being yelled at in all of this? How did we get here?

Over the next few days, I pulled back from talking to Hope, Monnie, and Christy in an effort to think on my own. I had been in this marriage for over three years, this last year being a toxic rollercoaster that seemed to spiral more and more downhill. I knew that I deserved better – but I also knew that I hadn't considered counseling. I couldn't stand the sight of my husband at that time, but I also wanted to do what was the appropriate course of action from a spiritual perspective. I told my husband and the minister of music from my church that I agreed to do spiritual counseling.

During that time, I would go into the office around 6:00 a.m. so that I could achieve the same amount of productivity before leaving around 5:00 p.m. for counseling. I had just started on a new team about seven months prior and didn't want to make a bad impression by slowing down my output.

Though counseling gave us an opportunity to talk with a mediator, I couldn't help but feel that most of the onus was being put on me. I was instructed to pray for him and to anoint his head while he was sleeping. I was told to be silent and soft when he was angered to wrath. The story I was given to model after spoke of a woman, married to a soon-to-be-prophet, who endured being locked out of the house and sleeping on the porch, only to meekly make her husband breakfast the next morning. I was told to not badger him if he wanted to leave the house and return home late and instead pray and anoint the house while he was gone.

Sheesh. These were really the things I was being counseled to do. It was sick.

We had been in counseling for a few months by the time I found myself on the floor sobbing and screaming.

On this particular day, I had found out that though my husband had allegedly been working hard in the online graduate program he had been enrolled in since August, he had gotten a zero GPA both semesters and was being kicked out of school. Schooling that I should have been able to trust that he had been participating in for the past several months. I was grinding. I was trying. I was encouraging. I was going to counseling. I was the cosigner on those graduate school loans. Man – what else was I supposed to do?!

I felt so fatigued. I remember just letting out a loud scream that I had pent up for years. I started rambling off things that I wouldn't revisit again until two years later when I was on a therapist's couch in San Francisco.

I yelled about how I had no idea how it felt to leave things up to someone else to fix. How I never had that luxury. How I didn't have the luxury of just giving up. How giving up was never an option for me. Because I had to stay alert and protect myself and provide for myself.

I yelled that I had no idea how it felt to lay my head in my mother's breast and have her rock me to peace, letting me know that everything would be alright.

I sobbed and sobbed. I said that I didn't know how it felt to lay my head on anyone's breast. That I had no idea what that felt like, but that I'd love to know how that felt. Oh, how much I wanted for someone to be strong enough... willing enough... in tune with me enough to know that I needed help... protection... LOVE.

I melted to the floor of my dining room and just screamed. I screamed and wept. Wept and screamed. Not fully realizing at that time that I was crying at the absence of my mother, the disappointment in my father, and the wrongdoing of family members. I was crying at the deceit of my husband and the collapse of my marriage.

I felt so sorry for myself, and for a second I just

wanted to be okay with being broken. Because I was too tired to be anything else. I was so keen to know how it would feel to have someone else pick up the pieces in my life. For me to not even try to put it together and for someone else to stand in for me. I gave up, and no one did this – I was so tired that I was okay with that, too.

My forehead was low to the hardwood floor as a puddle of tears began forming. Time had been warped. I don't know if it had been minutes, seconds, or longer. I was lost somewhere between infancy and present. Past and future.

Aaron's feet came into my limited line of sight as I sobbed on the floor. He was making his way to the door.

"I want a divorce," he yelled. "Do you hear me? I want a divorce! Your ass is crazy."

He stood there for a while, waiting for a response. I had nothing. Not for him. I just kept my head down and cried for myself. He opened the door, and he left.

While I couldn't find humor in it at the time, it's

almost comical how half-assed his reversals of blame and playing victim had become. We had moved from pretend prayers to Jesus to full-blown, "This is your fault, Casey." He came back later that day saying that he didn't mean what he had said. That he was just angry. What he was angry about – I'm not even sure. He said that he didn't want to be treated like a child and questioned about the things that he was doing... or not doing.

Our marriage had become such a circus at that point. In our spiritual counseling sessions, he was getting reinforcement that it was my responsibility to pray the evil spirits away, yet he was becoming more and more angry, with no attempt at change. By this time, his pores wreaked of alcohol every single day.

A month later, I was so over it. When I looked at call logs on the Verizon bill, I saw that the same pattern with the other woman had picked back up. He obviously never knew that his phone activity would show up in the bills. I never told him that I had confronted the other woman. But in June, I was done. I was literally done. I called to advise my counselor even before I let my husband know. I stated that I was making my decision even if the counselor felt the Lord would be unpleased. Regardless of what church leaders might think – this was insanity. It was clear that I was being taken advantage of, and I was over it.

I do remember the counselor urging me not to confront Aaron about this alone. I was asked to wait until the next counseling session, but I honestly didn't want to wait. Nor did I trust that anyone was really sane in all of this.

That night turned out to be violently explosive. It indeed signaled the end. But I didn't foresee just how explosive things would become.

I did not speak to Aaron for a whole year after seeing him in the courtroom during the restraining order hearing. I changed my phone number, I changed my work email address, I deleted my social media. The one thing that I did keep intact was my personal email address. I had so much of my life tied to that address, I was hesitant to change it with all the other change that I was forced to endure.

Aaron would reach out daily for a very long time. I had his emails sent to spam, but I did find some peace in being able to keep somewhat of a pulse check on his mental state. If he were to ever find out where I was or to become defiant enough to try to find me, I hoped that I would be able to at least get wind of it in his messaging. But I would not respond to him.

After a full year of legal separation, I was finally eligible to file for divorce. I needed to find his address so that he could be served the divorce papers. I didn't know what number to reach him on. I had terminated both of our old numbers that had been tied to our Verizon account when we were together.

With knots in my chest, I called Aaron's oldest sister.

"Hello?"

At the sound of her voice, ten years of memories flooded through my mind. Smiles, hugs, late nights of girl talk and wine. The pain on her face the last time I saw her that day in the court room.

"Hey, Nairobi."

"Casey?!"

I could hear the breath leave Nairobi's body as she said my name. She sobbed into the phone. I sobbed on the other end. We were both so happy to hear one another's voices after so much time had passed. Despite the circumstance, it was a beautiful reunion of sorts.

I didn't know what to expect, considering the quickness of the way I had dropped off the face of the earth. With the way I made a resolute decision to leave her brother. To start completely over in secret. To not look back, not even once, after so much time.

Nairobi expressed so much love for me from the other end of that phone. She let me know that she understood my stance. That she was so sorry that I had endured all that I had. She let me know that she didn't even recognize the person who had returned home to them after I had left. She didn't understand the darkness that was inside her brother. She didn't recognize it, but she knew that it was toxic and dangerous.

She assured me that she supported me and that I had done the right thing by leaving and securing my safety. She was proud of me.

I honestly didn't know what to expect from Nairobi. I didn't know what opinions there were of me, of the abrupt end to my marriage, or anything else. When I left Aaron, I left his family as well. I cut all ties. I didn't want to risk any measure of my safety. Nevertheless, feeling such genuine solidarity from a woman that I loved so much was soul-stirring. As much numbness as I had found in being disconnected, talking with Nairobi and learning that she believed that I did the right thing was love. It was *love*. In the fullest essence of the word. It was love.

Nairobi gave me Aaron's number. And we ended our call.

I took several deeps breath, attempting to prepare myself for the next call I was about to make.

I went and sat on the couch, trying to position myself in an upright position that would give my tone strength.

No, no, no. I shook my head and sat Indian style on the couch, trying to chill myself out a bit. I took in another deep sigh.

I looked at the phone, still not being able to hit the green phone dial icon.

I stood up and walked into my bedroom, closing the door.

What am I doing? I'm in a one-bedroom apartment. What additional privacy is there to be found in shutting the door when you're already alone, Casey?

Whatever – I just went with it. Standing up, in my bedroom, with the door closed, I made the call.

Aaron answered the phone and my heart fell to my feet. What used to be the sweetest sound in the whole wide world now brought me so much pain and trauma. Anger and hurt replaced that capacity in my chest.

"Hello... hello?"

I clinched my teeth together.

"Hey, Aaron, it's Casey."

"Casey... baby... baby, I'm so sorry..."

Aaron went on to apologize over and over again. Telling me that he was a better man that day than he had ever been. That he had spent so many years trying to be bigger for me. Trying to do all the things that he thought that I would want him to do... trying to be all the things that he thought I would want for him to be. He said that he finally wanted all those things for himself.

"You hurt me, Aaron. You physically *hurt* me."

I could hear Aaron get choked up on the other end of the phone.

"I know. And I'm so sorry, Casey. For a long time, I didn't even remember that night. I was so out of it... so drunk... it's like I blacked out. Sometime after it happened, I remembered all the things that I did, and I hated myself for it."

Aaron went on to tell me that he was struggling with some demons long before we ever got married. Demons that he had always tried to hide from me. He wanted to overcome his struggles on his own.

"There were times that you would come home from work and ask me if I had been drinking and, being the loving wife that you were, you would believe whatever I said. I'd tell you that I had only had a few beers, but, baby, I was bad off. I was struggling with a habit I couldn't kick. And it got more and more out of control."

Being the loving wife that I was? I was naïve as hell. I could even say that I was silly. In the first months of our marriage, I was paying some bills and asked Aaron for his credit card online passcode to pay his bill while I was at it. Once he gave it to me, I logged in and saw the same store listed every single day – sometimes twice a day. *ABC Store $8.64, ABC Store $9.94, ABC Store $9.13.*

In Charlotte, liquor stores are owned and managed by the county, and they are all called ABC stores. I thought that was strange. I was at work when this happened. That same day, I went on a walk with a coworker of mine who was married and some years older than I. She was the only other black person on my team. She was like an instant big sister, being able to relate to me on so many things.

"Is it normal for Aaron to be going to the ABC store every single day to be buying a drink? Like, every single day?" I asked.

My coworker cocked her head back and looked at me with a frown.

"Girl, no! Every single day? The ABC store? Liquor every single day?"

"Hmph."

I asked Aaron about it later when I got home. He shrugged it off, saying that he liked to enjoy a drink to take the edge off every now and then. I let it go and honestly didn't think much more about it. I had never been exposed to patterns of addiction. I had never lived with Aaron before we got married. I was learning new behaviors. Learning a new normal.

Even in the years throughout our marriage when he would call me and make these grand proclamations about pouring a full bottle of liquor down the sink, I would be confused.

"Okaay… why did you do that?" I would ask –

honestly not understanding the underlying significance of those moments. That he was desperately and independently trying to kick a habit that he had. A habit that I didn't know existed.

I never even noticed him drink every day. This, I now understand, was by design as well. After we would host large functions, I'd notice that remaining liquor in our house could never last past a day or so. I naively thought that the situation was similar to a kid not being able to have candy or chips in the house without bingeing.

They say hindsight is always 20/20.

"Aaron, we're done. I do not want to be married to you. It's great that you are a better person, but you need to be that better person for yourself. It never needed to be for me. Your life goals should never be for another person. You're going to have to figure this thing out on your own. I'm done. I want a divorce, and I need your address so that the papers can be served to you."

Aaron went on to tell me that I was created for him. That I was his rib. He said that if we were to get back together, we would be a testimony to people. That we would show others how powerful love is and how true love can come back from anything.

I responded by telling Aaron that I'm a testimony *because* I left – and I meant that. I had no interest in revisiting the past. I wanted the best future for him. It's why I had asked the police to not arrest him and tarnish his record. But that future would have to be without me.

Aaron refused to give me his address in that conversation. I resorted to using his families' addresses, and he was eventually served the divorce papers. We got our divorce. And we continue to live separate lives.

14

OLD TIME RELIGION

"Stepped in the water, the water was cold." Anderson .Paak, "The Waters"

For a long time after I left my husband, I resented the church. I resented many of the teachings I had been indoctrinated with. I resented the leadership that had misguided so many women before me – women who had endured decades of mistreatment and violence for the sake of being "godly" wives. There are facets of religious construct that I still resent today, to be honest.

To be even more honest, I was brokenhearted. Deeper than resentment, I felt betrayed. I felt that my vulnerability and trust had been mishandled. I felt that I had been guided down a dangerous, destructive path by people that I had put so much faith and reverence in. The heartache and weariness from it all ran very deep. That pain still lingers.

I had been taught my entire life about how chaste and upright a woman should be. When my husband began cheating, it was him that the church protected. I was told that I needed to pray more, I needed to anoint his head while he slept, I needed to be soft-spirited and not pester him if he behaved indecently. It is truly disheartening that women are guided in that way.

In August 2019, I watched Jerrod Carmichael's HBO special, *Sermon on the Mount*, wherein I witnessed a pastor dish out the same toxic counsel that had been given to me after my husband's infidelity. Jerrod's mom had recently found out that her husband of many years had four children outside their marriage.

In the documentary, the pastor tells Jerrod's mom that "love hides a multitude of sins." The pastor works to convince Jerrod's mom that all of her husband's infidelities happened while he was "weak in the flesh," but that she should think about what leaving her husband would to do to him, the children, and the grandchildren. The pastor told her that the fact that her husband kept his infidelity from her for all those years was a sign that he was trying to protect his wife. It must have been terribly hard for the husband to come clean and admit these things.

This was warped logic... this tradition... was all too familiar. It triggered so much anger inside me. The messages from the pastor in the documentary were the same ones that are instilled in women throughout the churches that I grew up in and would frequent in the South. Women are taught to be chaste and long-suffering. Men are to be seen as forgivable and worthy of prestige no matter how horrible they treat their wives. Had the roles reversed, the same logic would not apply.

For years after leaving Charlotte, I could not even listen to a gospel song. I couldn't. There was so much tenderness there. There still is. I didn't even visit the inside of a church, for mistrust and fear around what leaders might encourage me to do... to be.

I had tried to follow the guidance of my spiritual counselor when Aaron and I were working to repair our marriage, even though the guidance I received went against my understanding of self-respect and love. I was afraid of being around people who would expect me to live in a box that I didn't agree with or fit inside of. I didn't want to be the type of woman that many pastors and traditions were guiding me to be.

I was tired of being misled by the people and institutions that I had put my faith in. I realized that not all churches are the same. That people take their own understanding of religion and twist it to fit their own agendas and beliefs. This understanding doesn't change my uneasiness around the matter. I am still in a journey of healing in this area of my life.

Up until the shattering of my marriage, I had spent my entire life being guided by the principles of my faith. I had done what I understood to be right. I poured my life into ministry. I did right by my husband. Yet, in the time where I rightfully said, "I choose to show myself the unconditional love that I know I deserve by leaving my husband," I was told that I would be breaking covenant to do so. I was told that my decisions were wayward. That I hadn't suffered long enough.

The weight of this experience is still so heavy for me. The hurt is still raw. The feedback that I received from the church acted as an element that allowed, even encouraged, more and more toxicity to fester in my marriage. Aaron actually knew, in a twisted way, that he was getting some leeway to be unfaithful based on the instruction that was being given to me.

I'm still angry that women are often guided in such a sick way. Woman are powerful; women are precious. Women so often carry more than they are given credit for. To be told to shrink and play a role that is small is unacceptable. It is unacceptable.

My experience has caused me to question everything about my religion, questioning whether a lot of what I have learned has been tradition or truth. It has caused me to reevaluate what true love is and how much of what I have seen has been anchored in bondage and susceptibility to abuse.

Of course, I don't have all the answers. I am still learning and relearning things that I thought I knew, every single day. I'm still absorbing truths of the world. I am traveling and observing cultures. Observing people. Observing family and community constructs. Taking a deeper look at love and surveying truth.

This period of uncertainty is something that I'm comfortable in, to be honest. I'm okay not having to put a label on anything so that others feel satisfied. I'm happy to not have to proclaim a particular regimen of religion or be pressured to check off certain routines so that those around me can validate that I'm fitting into a box they approve of.

Being in California makes my period of healing and self-discovery easier. I can believe in and revere God, gawk at the magnificence of the well-balanced universe that I am in, be thankful for all the goodness that has transpired in my life, and do good in the world – without feeling pressured to answer to people about what belief system I fit into, as is common back in the South. I am grateful for the freedom to be. To live. To heal. And maybe one day… to love again. In the way that I feel is healthiest for me.

I remember my first time listening to a gospel song after leaving Charlotte. It is funny how something seemingly small can stand out as being so significant… when it's anchored in so much symbolism. It was Christmas of 2017, eighteen months after my move. Eighteen months since the entire routine of my life had changed. Eighteen months since I'd stepped a single foot in a church.

My Uncle Reggie and his wife had flown in from Alabama to visit me in Oakland. My best friend, Monnie, flew in from Los Angeles to spend Christmas with us as well.

Reggie and I were discussing music, like we always do. We played various songs that we loved, putting each other onto the latest favorites that we had. It was beautiful. Reggie asked me if I had heard "Change Me" by Tamela Mann.

I thought on whether I wanted to tell him that I didn't really want to hear it. That I didn't want to hear anything that would remind me of church. That there was a still a rawness there that I barely knew how to adequately articulate, let alone explore.

I didn't want to tell him how sad listening to the song would make me feel. How angry it might make me feel.

"I haven't heard it," I said.

He played it.

Change me oh God / Make me more like you
Change me oh God / Wash me through and through

As the song played, I immediately began to cry. It was painful to revisit that part of myself. That part that connected so much to spirituality and Christian faith. That part of me that would leave all my cares and fears and hopes and hurts in songs and messages such as these.

I cried because the words were beautiful. And pure. The song hugged me tightly. It seemed to whisper to me that there was refuge someplace outside myself. Tamela's voice… that style of music was more than familiar. My roots were tangled all up in it. I cried and rocked… cried and rocked.

After the song ended, the room fell silent. Everyone was watching me, trying to understand what I was feeling. Monnie likely knew. She understood how much I had avoided these types of encounters. How there was so much that I was unsure of. How disappointed I was with the way that the church had handled me. But how much of my existence had been intertwined in ministry and singing and praise and love for God. I rocked back and forth, biting my lip… trying to figure out what to say.

I tried to express to my uncle the very things that I still struggle to articulate today. The fact that I feel disappointed and hurt by the religious construct that I had loved and depended on so much. The fact that I resent many of the things that I had been taught about what a woman's nature should be and how those teachings often perpetuate cycles of abuse and battered self-esteem. I tried to articulate how I was still in a place where I was working to be comfortable with vulnerability again, even within the context of my faith. But that I just wasn't in a place where I was ready to be so unguarded again.

As I mentioned, I still don't have the answers on this. I am still working my way through healing and openness to religion. I believe there is a power that has been protecting me and guiding me. I believe there is purpose for me, and, time and time again, I have been blessed to follow through on that purpose. I believe that events in my life are more than just randomness and that prayers are answered.

There are ideals I still struggle to reconcile as it relates to my faith, such as the weaponizing of Christianity in the advancement of racism and the roles traditionally forced upon women in the constructs of religious systems. I'm in no rush to jump to an answer on it all. I am absolutely grateful to be in a space where I can have the freedom to survey and learn.

With time, I know that I will come to the place of healing and find more completeness in this area of my life. I do hope to one day have peace and resolution around it all. Today, I don't have the answers, but I have learned that that is okay.

15

THE BAY

"All the things I thought I knew, I'm learning them again." –
India.Arie, "Heart of the Matter"

Starting my life over in the Bay Area turned out to
be incredible. I arrived in this new city, completely
unsure of my plans and questioning everything about
my identity: my core values, my faith, my place in

society as a woman, my beliefs around relationships. I had believed that I was so sure about so many things before circumstances brought me to my new home ... before my entire world changed.

When I showed up to the Bay Area, however, I was certain about nothing. Nothing except the fact that I was mad as hell at the people and circumstances that had catapulted me into my current state (myself included). I vowed that I would offer myself the grace to explore everything that my heart desired. I vowed that I would not let people's opinions or selfish desires block me from coming to understand what *I* believed was truth. I wanted to be okay with changing my mind, time and time again if I needed to. This time, my path would be my own choosing.

In the Bay area, I found the space and support to do just that. The people that surrounded me were so liberal. They expressed themselves in bold, audacious ways. Outside my office building in San Francisco, I could witness full-fledged protests right in front of me. Walking down any given street, there was vibrant cultural expression – in wardrobe, in hairstyles, in art, in music, in festivals, in words spoken. It was a melting pot that allowed the authenticity of individual culture to shine through. I had never witnessed such genuine diversity – it was empowering.

In the early days of living in the Bay Area, I went to a powerful event in Oakland at Alena Museum. Tunde Wey, a Nigerian immigrant chef, hosted the event as part of his *Blackness in America* dinner series for which he had traveled across more than eight major cities across the country. In these settings, Tunde Wey created familial environments where locals of the African diaspora would sit together, eating family-style, having candid conversations about the state of Blackness in the United States. Chef Tunde was curating these conversations because he wanted to discuss race in America from the perspectives of Black people. The discourse that was created in that room through the prompts given and questions raised was jaw-dropping. It was healthy.

It was affirmation that we as a people are no monolith, and that each of our perspectives are equally as important. Our unique experiences should be heard and digested – by each of us, not merely those who are outside our race.

The meal consisted of pepper soup, quail stew, dodo, efo rice, jollof, frejon and puff puff. Though my paternal grandfather is Nigerian – we are Igbo – it was my first time eating many of these cultural dishes. The spirit of the room and the act of sharing the meal were moving in and of themselves. I was so hungry to absorb a better understanding of the culture… of the community that surrounded me… of myself.

There was a brother who spoke from his lens of Blackness in America, having been violated by a group of Black men for no apparent reason in the first few weeks of his residency in America. He had been walking down the street when a white van pulled up beside him. He asked the people in the van for directions to a building he was attempting to locate. Someone pointed him in one direction, and as he gazed off to look, the door of the van swung open and multiple people jumped out, beating him with their fists and feet. Black men, the same color as he, had beaten him.

Many of us in the room shook our heads in understanding. *Ah, that must have been some sort of gang initiation.* It was interesting that many of us, almost in concert, knew what that scene must have represented, as if it should have made apparent sense. For the person who was attacked, this was a disgusting and unwarranted display of violence, and he was having a hard time shaking the bitterness of that experience. He desired to reconcile his own experiences of Blackness in America with the perspectives shared by others.

In a manner that was just as thought provoking, a woman spoke boldly under the tagline "The Black Woman is God." Karen Seneferu was her name. I had never heard a proclamation so controversial yet demanding. She spoke of strengths and gifts that rested inside me... inside many of us in that room. She gave praise to the womb of the African woman and spoke of history in a manner that I'd never heard broken down in such a way. It was *life*.

Another brother – a preacher and poet by the

name of Marvin K. White – read a poem centered on a matriarch. I believe it was a piece from his collection of poetry called *Our Name Be Witness*. The poem was engrossing. We all became lost in it – the smells, visuals, tastes that he sketched out with his words – but what surprised me most was that he actually cursed during the poem. The Southern belle in me was shooketh! *Ha!* I let out a laugh when he did it… one that stayed with me the rest of the night.

The owner of Alena Museum described the purpose of the venue, emphasizing the importance of him owning that property in the face of the gentrification that impacted the Bay Area – Oakland, specifically. He described that in the African language of Tigrinya, "Alena" translates to "We are here." He went on to describe the importance of preserving the things that are "black as fuck" and reveling in how beautiful that is. Those words moved me deeply. It was a representation of self-love and authenticity I hadn't quite experienced in such an unrestrained way.

Another woman stood up, speaking about how her students struggled with the idea of remaining peaceful in a climate where their lives were being threatened by the very authorities charged with protecting them. She mentioned how pained they were to be targeted simply because of the color of their skin. These students would come to her, asking how they could take part in the change that was so desperately needed in the country.

The woman's stated response sent shivers through my soul. Her words still serve as a light to me today. They are words that I echo to my mentees.

"Your very body in places where you are underrepresented is protest. Your nose. Your lips. The rhythm in your speech is protest. Because you show up, because you occupy shared spaces – you are making a bold stride for progress. Don't hide. Don't cover. Take your blackness with you in every environment. Be big. Be unapologetic. Your existence is protest."

I remember calling my father that night with so much excitement, recounting all the amazing things I had witnessed. Describing the stark difference in tone that this new region of the country had in comparison to any other place I had been. It made me feel alive. More alive than I had ever felt before.

The Bay Area continued to be this fertile ground for growth and awakening for me. There was never a shortage of intellectual dialogue to take part in. There was always a vibrant festival or celebration to attend, exposing me to traditions and history very different from those I had been told about at previous points in my life.

Comparatively speaking, I'd describe my growth as being exponential in this new place. Here, it was okay for me to question. It was okay for me to try new things completely outside of anything I could have ever imagined before. I wasn't asked whether I had gone to church on Sunday. No one asked me if I was married and having kids. No one cared if I wore heels to the club or sneakers. People just *were* in the Bay. I was able to just *be*.

I was killing it at my job, but I never needed to talk about it. I was living comfortably in my lifestyle, but it never needed to be a qualifier for social groups. In this new environment, it was easy to just vibe with people from all walks of life. You could just as easily be five months into an acquaintanceship without realizing the person that you'd been hanging out with in your circle of acquaintances owned sixteen patents and was paying $4,000 in rent.

It was incredible!

There was just as much variety in my dating experiences in the Bay Area, which I appreciated. When I arrived, I had no idea what the right "type" for me needed to be. I had realized that a person "having potential," while commendable, wasn't good enough. I had grown to understand that a person being motivated by the things that would seem to please me (rather than a life they innately wanted for themselves) wasn't healthy.

Outside of the things that I knew I *wasn't* looking for, I wasn't dead set on a list of what a guy needed to have. This was a good thing, because I wanted to explore. The Bay Area was ripe for doing so.

I no longer believed that there was such a thing as a soul mate. I believed that there were amazing people all over the world who could be a nice match for another person for a myriad of reasons. Someone could migrate from one part of the country to another, possessing the same traits, only to stumble across several compatible companions. And while I no longer believed in a soul mate, I did desire great times exploring and learning about myself.

Learning about myself – I did! *Ha.* There was this one brother who my friends and I would call iRobot. We would really refer to him as such in our girl's chat. Here's the thing: I didn't allow for my dating experiences to develop into anything of permanency. It was too soon for any of that. And I *definitely* didn't plan on introducing the guys that I dated to anyone important in my life. So I would label the guys that I dated with thematic nicknames to jog my friends' memories about a given guy's persona.

The iRobot chapter was an interesting one. And there was never a dull moment with him. On paper, this brother was something out of a novel! *50 Shades of*

Grey to be exact. He was so Christian Grey. He was a brilliant engineer, confident, had swagger like no other – and was *fine*. Most of the sexiness that he gave off came from his persona. He was just the shit.

iRobot matched my feistiness and was quicker in wit. If I ever had a dig at him, he could take it without flinching, squint his eyes, and throw something back that would make me raise an eyebrow. I loved to banter with him.

We had the best of times. Never in my life had I experienced so much spontaneity with another person. There would be days that I would literally leave my car at a Best Buy or some other random place for a Friday night of bar hopping and not think to go back and pick it up until days later.

Geeking out with him was the best as well. We could watch documentaries for hours on a Sunday and spend hours more dissecting them. iRobot was cool – he fed my desire for excitement and thrill. It was dope to know that such a high was possible. He also happened to be selfish and self-absorbed, which eventually caused that chapter to close – but it was fun, nevertheless.

Thaddeus, I would say, was on the opposite end of the spectrum. Though my friends grew to know his actual name, in the beginning he was referred to as Serendipity. I wasn't supposed to fall for him as much as I did; I wasn't supposed to develop substantial feelings for anyone. But he was a beautiful surprise.

I met him when I went to play basketball with a group of acquaintances. He was cool enough when I met him at the start of the game – but his swagger on the court was noticeable. I knew nothing about basketball, but like so many other things during this time of my life, I was trying out something new.

I would see Serendipity at different times thereafter, but I wouldn't interact with him at any real length. It was at a day party in Oakland that our start at dating occurred. Serendipity was at the party, and as I walked past him, *acting* as if I was really going to walk past without speaking, he gently grabbed my hand – just as I knew he would.

After one flirtatious comment after another, he asked if he could have my number. I obliged. Soon after that, we commenced on our dating journey with a chemistry that was rare. I had effortlessly opened up to this man about my life, my past, and my scars. He had the longest arms, which would swallow me up and soothe me as we talked while sitting on a pier or taking a hike. After a few dates, I saved his number in my phone, naming him Serendipity. It was funny – I actually told him what his name was in my phone after I saved it. The fact that it was a compliment perhaps made it less offensive. I don't know, I didn't ask.

As I previously conveyed, Serendipity had the most nurturing and beautiful spirit. He was steady and consistent in that. It was something that I could always count on, though he was not the most adventurous and outgoing. He was very much a homebody and selectively social, which I would find underwhelming at times – although his compassion was welcomed and appreciated.

Other guys that I have dated have been at different points along the continuum between iRobot and Serendipity, all bringing personalities and interactions that taught me something about myself. Dating gave me insight into the things that I could probably live with and the things that I absolutely could not. They also brought in relativity. While one thing might seem intolerable initially, I'd sometimes realize that the antipathy associated with one trait could turn out to be nothing compared to the horrid trait of another.

Dating in the Bay Area, much like every other experience in the region, was diverse and edifying. I was able to take my time in exploring things I chose – with no pressure around leaning toward one school of thought or another.

Over three years in, the Bay Area has continued to be a place that I sincerely enjoy. I learn from my environment and the people in it every day. I am ever-evolving, ever-seeking, ever-growing. I am absolutely grateful that a spontaneous decision turned out to be such a perfect choice.

16

FINDING FREEDOM

"You wanna fly, you got to give up the shit that weighs you down."
Toni Morrison, "Song of Solomon"

My journey of digging deep and unpacking my foundational experiences was one of the most difficult things I have ever done. I had to learn how to sit with my pain, my sadness, and my hurt long enough to understand them. This willingness to accept fragility was nurturing to my soul. It helped me accept the realities that have shaped my identity. It helped me be vocal about the things that I needed from my loved ones – because I was worthy of being seen and valued.

Acknowledging my pain and frailties has not taken anything away from the strength I have. On the contrary, it has amplified the gifts and authenticity that I am able to exude every single day. The genuine freedom and openness that I have found has bled over into every facet of my life. This new feeling of weightlessness has inspired me to do less compartmentalizing in my life. It has given me boldness to just *be*.

In the office, in my community, on the stage, with my friends – I am unapologetically alive today. I am bold in showing all of me, all of the magic that results from my personal lens and experiences. I've always been a high-performer, I've always been forward – but I stand in even more vulnerable truth today. I stand in unguarded freedom. As a result, my purpose is louder... my message is more honest than it has ever been.

In whatever I lay my hand to, I am intentional about creating space for those who have traditionally been cast off from certain opportunities as the result of stigma or lack of access. In so many instances, that person could have been me. Yet I am proof that people have the ability to defy statistics. I am also proof that those same people do not have to pretend as if their differences, trauma, or lack are nonexistent for the sake of achievement.

In every facet of my life, I use my voice and stature to speak boldly about the experiences that have shaped me – domestic violence, mental illness, loss, womanhood, and pain. This is for my family, my friends, my company, and my community. In October 2019, I was asked to be one of two speakers on a panel discussion directed towards the top 100 executives in my global business organization. I was asked to share my story of moving across the country to find safety after experiencing domestic violence, and I shed light on the importance of executives being fortresses of support for their people.

I seized the opportunity to be transformative. I know that this is my purpose and gift. Instead of this robotic shell I was trapped in during my previous life, I was *real.* The rhythm in my voice, the confidence in my tone, the style in which I conveyed my message was authentic. And it was a wake-up call to those executives. The conversation ended with a standing ovation and a room full of tears.

One executive came to me and said, "Casey, your story is so much bigger than this company. It is big enough to touch the world."

I smiled so big, for that was something that I was already well aware of. And on this side of my pain, on this side of my experiences, I didn't need an invitation or permission to reach out to the world. I didn't need to ration out pieces of myself to make sure that it was digestible to those who might engage with me in varying environments. I had come to understand the power of my experiences. That plan to touch the world was already in motion.

I am everything that I am because of my

experiences, not in spite of them. I am beautiful, I am deep. I am complex, I am rich in spirit. I am empathetic, I am strong. After previously questioning so many things about what I should have done, I've landed at a place of sincere gratitude for everything that my experiences have cultivated inside me. I am everything that I should be.

Despite my fears, the abrupt departure from Charlotte did not stifle my career progression. My taking a leave of absence to invest in my mental health did not hamper my trajectory. About fourteen months after returning to the office, I received yet another promotion, earning it after hard work, leadership, and exceeding performance expectations.

Today, I am proud to be a voice in my company on matters outside the strong work I do around revenue generation. I serve as a vocal member on the Global Diversity & Inclusion Council. I am on the leadership team of the Northern California chapter of an Employee Resource Group (ERG). I have mobilized change in metrics that relate to providing access to underrepresented cohorts of people in my line of business. These are things that are important to me. These are passions that I tap into in all facets of my life.

I am grateful to be enjoying a rich life in my community, planning events and investing in people as much as I can. In August 2019, I spoke at a +150-person, two-day ERG Summit – advising Black and Latinx Employee Resource Group leaders at various companies on how to gain and maximize executive sponsorship. My push to them was to lean into all connections with authenticity. To shed the burden of trying to figure out how to emulate the homogenous cultures that surround them and to stand in passion and truth. That transformative approach makes all the difference.

I mentor college students and young professionals year-round, happily working to help save them years of learning how to navigate certain personal and career-related terrains on their own. I ask them to name their fears and insecurities, to be cognizant of them – and to combat them from the inside out. To be audacious and bold.

I perform fairly often these days. My most recent performance was at a Juneteenth Celebration, singing "Four Women" by Nina Simone. I was intentional about this song choice, as it was a corporate event co-sponsored by my company and two other tech companies in the area, hosting more than 200 people. It was an event that I created the partnership for and helped orchestrate, in a successful attempt to bring authenticity and genuine celebration of Black culture within my company.

I wanted for the culture and stories represented in that song to be heard and felt by all in attendance, no matter their ethnicity. That is important for me – living in truth and freedom. I will not choose to be anywhere where my freedom is not protected, celebrated, and supported. I owe that much to myself. We all do.

The Chicago Marathon? I finally ran those 26.2 miles! In 2016, that dream was halted by the violent end to my marriage and the reconstruction of my life.

In 2017, my battle with depression inhibited me from a second attempt. In 2018, I was able to face that glorious feat… with my mind and spirit intact.

On October 7, 2018, I flew to Chicago and met my friend and former coworker Jessica. She had relocated from Charlotte to New York and was ecstatic to be by my side as I embarked on my first marathon. I was thrilled to have her running the marathon with me and offering me tips on making it through the long run. She recommended that I dedicate each mile to something in my life that was important to me so that I would always have motivation during my run when I needed it.

Jessica suggested that I be very intentional about choosing things that would propel me forward throughout the miles that would be especially tough and painful. I created my list and tucked it into the pocket of my armband.

1. *Casey*
2. *Resilience*
3. *Fearlessness*
4. *Freedom*

5. *Self-love*

6. *Starting again*

7. *My grandfather*

8. *Forgiveness*

9. *Finding my voice*

10. *Healing*

11. *Making my support system proud*

12. *Triumph after not giving up*

13. *My mommy*

14. *Grinding through it*

15. *MBA*

16. *Shattering statistics*

17. *Domestic violence awareness*

18. *C-Suite*

19. *Happiness*

20. *Doing the impossible*

21. *Making room for minorities*

22. *Standing up for myself*

23. *Delayed gratification*

24. *Big Ma*

25. *Name in lights*

26. *Finishing what I started <3*

It's fair to be wondering what, if anything, happened between my Aunt Rose and I in all this. Whether or not I tried to have another moment of reckoning with her. Whether I took action to absolve the pain that I felt around her treatment towards me.

The answer is that I had already stopped communicating with Aunt Rose before my depression struck in 2017. Soon after arriving to California, I had come to a decision to no longer accept her toxicity in my life. Before my move, I would step through the motions of an outwardly normal family dynamic with her as much as I could. It always felt like the right thing to do. The righteous thing to do.

We still lived in close proximity to one another even after I was out of her house and living with my new mom, father, and siblings. We'd interact at church, award ceremonies, and occasional family functions. Her antics never waned, though they were fewer by the time I moved to Charlotte – mostly because I had less reason to interact with her. Admittedly, it never became easier to stomach her behaviors, but I chose to swallow the difficulty and hurt from my interactions with her even as I stepped into adulthood. I felt that I was tough enough to do so.

When I moved to California, however, I had the last straw. Before leaving, I made it clear to my parents that I did not want Aunt Rose to know where I was headed. I was leaving quietly and in a hurry for my safety, and I did not want Aunt Rose to have any power to jeopardize that. About a month into me living in California, a person from my high school who was contracting with my company reached out through our internal messenger system to let me know that his dad (who lived in South Carolina) told him that I was living in California. This person wanted to know if Aaron and I were okay.

You can imagine the panic and frustration that went through me. I reached out to my parents to ask if they had mentioned anything to Aunt Rose. Low and behold, my dad confessed to her that I had moved to California after she had asked him over and over. He had believed that Aunt Rose was genuinely

concerned for my well-being. I argued that
throughout my entire life, she had never once cared
for my well-being and that I was determined to
protect myself, even if he wouldn't. I told him I was
changing my number and that he was not to give it to
her – if he did, I would change it again and not give it
to either of them.

I was angry in that moment, but I have never
regretted the decision to rid myself of the poison of
that relationship. I didn't care to go back and forth
around what happened. What was clear to me in that
moment was that I had a chance to choose what I
would allow in my life. That moment for me was life
or death, and I had a right to protect myself in
whatever way that I deemed necessary.

After a three-year silence with my Aunt Rose, I
broke it. I went to South Carolina and paid her a visit
when she became ill. I love her. I always will. I want
goodness and health for her. I made sure I expressed
that. But I could not allow an ongoing,
communicative relationship with her. When I
returned to California, I continued in the state of

disconnection that I had established. I am content with that stance and am all the better for it.

Will I find love again? I'm not sure. Potentially... with time. To be honest, I believe that my heart is still a bit broken. I'm still not comfortable resting in a state of vulnerability with another person. My heart is still not in a place where it is ready to trust... ready to let down its guard.

I'm okay with not being ready today and finally admitting that I'm fragile. I'm okay with recognizing that I'm broken in certain areas. I'm okay with naming it. Giving it sunlight. And protecting it until it heals.

Today, I am happy to be in a place where my life truly feels full. Rather than ignoring elements of my truth, hoping they dissipate if I suffocate them long enough, I've learned how to sit with myself. To ask for what I need. To know that it is okay to need.

Though my process was one hell of a rollercoaster, I have found a state of being that is both rich and priceless. I have stepped through a lot of pain, some of which still lingers, yet I am existing in a form of weightlessness. An ease that makes something as simple as breathing in and out a little lighter than before.

Today, I am actually free.

ACKNOWLEDGEMENTS

For providing the support and resources to aid in one of the toughest transitions of my life, I owe many thanks to Ann Lowe, Tiffany Lee, Mark Godfriaux, JB Meanor, Chuck Hagel, Patrick Martin, Whitley Harrison, David Harrison and George Johnson.

For editing my manuscript in its earliest stages and every iteration after, pulling the very best out of me, and helping to produce the powerful work that you now hold in your hands, I owe endless thanks to Courtney Castor.

For providing tireless ears, encouragement, valuable feedback, and unconditional love that helped fuel me as I worked so hard to bring my vision to fruition – endless thanks to my family, Chinaka Albert Diké, Laketa Diké, Corey Diké, and Reginald Lowe.

For speaking life into me over and over and over again as I stepped through the emotional rollercoaster of finishing my book this year, I thank my beautiful friends Aja Thornton and Andrew Robinson.

For lifting me every single day since I fled across the country in search of a new life and freedom, I must thank my very best friends, Monnie and Hope. Their love runs deeper than deep, and I couldn't have asked for better partners in crime.

For sowing enough love, legacy, and light inside me to last an entire lifetime – I thank my mother, Wanda Denise Lowe Diké. I am so very grateful that her spirit lives on in me.

Casey Richardson is a current resident of Oakland, California. Casey's greatest hope is to deposit the best of herself into the world – to change it for the better if at all possible. When Casey's life is over, she hopes to have left something behind that is good and perpetual – just as her mother miraculously did for her.